T0329389

Death of a Discipline?

Reflections on the history, state, and future of Social Anthropology in Zimbabwe

Munyaradzi Mawere & Artwell Nhemachena

Langaa Research & Publishing CIG
Mankon, Bamenda

Publisher:
Langaa RPCIG
Langaa Research & Publishing Common Initiative Group
P.O. Box 902 Mankon
Bamenda
North West Region
Cameroon
Langaagrp@gmail.com
www.langaa-rpcig.net

Distributed in and outside N. America by African Books Collective
orders@africanbookscollective.com
www.africanbookscollective.com

ISBN-10: 9956-762-81-4

ISBN-13: 978-9956-762-81-1

© Munyaradzi Mawere & Artwell Nhemachena 2017

Table of Contents

Chapter 1

Anthropology, Society, and Change in Conversation

Knowledge of anthropology enables us to look with greater freedom at the problems confronting our civilisation (Franz Uri Boas[1] 1928)

The scope of anthropology

The question on what anthropology really is and is not is notoriously complex and confusing. Many people, even some students of anthropology, when asked this question remain mum, with some confusing it with its sister discipline of sociology. This being the case, it is more important than not to clarify to our readers what anthropology is and is not, right from the outset.

---

[1] Franz Uri Boas was a German-American anthropologist and a pioneer of modern anthropology who is now considered as the "Father of American Anthropology". Though Boas became an anthropologist by occupation after his expedition to the Eskimo country, he was a physicist by training as he graduated with a PhD in physics from the University of Kiel (German) in 1881. Boas was one of the most prominent opponents of the then popular ideologies of scientific racism, the idea that race is a biological concept and that human behaviour is best understood through the typology of biological characteristics. In a series of ground studies of skeletal anatomy he showed that cranial shape and size was highly malleable depending on environmental factors such as health and nutrition, in contrast to the claims by racial anthropologists of the day that held head shape to be a stable racial trait. Boas also worked to demonstrate that differences in human behaviour are not primarily determined by innate biological dispositions, but are largely a result of cultural differences acquired through social learning.

The word 'anthropology' was first used in English as early as 1593. It derives from the Greek word *'anthropos'* which designates human/man and *'logos'* which means to study. As a distinct academic discipline, anthropology is relatively young, with its genealogy traceable to the intellectual enlightenment of the 18th and early 19th centuries in Europe and North America.

Basing on the roots of the word, anthropology studies humankind in all its diversity or from a holistic perspective: it is the study of mankind in its widest sense both as social and cultural beings. This means that anthropology is concerned explicitly and directly with the study of all kinds of people of all periods around the world, not only those within a limited area and time. For scholars like Kroeber (1948), anthropology is 'the science of groups of men, and their behaviour and productions.' In a more or less similar fashion, Ember and Ember (1990: 2) define anthropology as a 'discipline of infinite curiosity about human beings'. In fact, anthropology generally studies human biology and culture in a bid to understand what defines humans as such and why humans are what they are. As Ember and Ember elaborate, anthropologists seek answers to an enormous variety of questions about humans which include but not limited to: when, where, and why humans appeared on earth, how and why societies in the past present have varied in their customary ideas and practices. Yet, understood as such, some people become even more confused especially as they try to understand how then anthropology differ from other such disciplines as biology, history, philosophy, sociology, among others; disciplines that in some respects also study human biology and cultures. Also, other people would want to know why anthropology specialises in understanding human behaviour, aspects of human experience, productions and cultures. Responding to the latter question, one should understand that the realm of culture had been largely neglected by the other sciences such as political science, sociology, history, and psychology. On how anthropology distinguishes itself, we underscore that anthropology differs from other such disciplines as philosophy, history, and biology in that its approach to the study of humanity is holistic in so far as it is interested in understanding the biological and cultural aspects of humankind around the world throughout time and cross-cultural comparisons. The multi-faceted or holistic nature, focus, and methods of anthropology used in studying human beings also distinguish it [anthropology] from other disciplines. Besides, these tenets allow anthropology to act as a bridge between other sciences and humanities. Understood as such, anthropology is expected to play a positive and constructive role in any society, whether a rapidly changing society or not. This is because 'real' anthropologists always pose critical questions for themselves such as: 'What approaches can one expect regarding the interaction between anthropologists and society?; Will these approaches keep us [anthropologists] from repeating the mistakes of the past [colonial] anthropologists?' Though these questions will be discussed in detail in chapter 2, we underline here that the first step towards the direction of becoming constructively involved in rigorous and serious researches without repeating the mistakes of the past anthropologists is to be truly reflexive and self-introspective in practising anthropology.

As an umbrella discipline, anthropology comprises of five broad subjects namely; physical/biological anthropology, anthropological linguistics, applied anthropology, archaeology, and cultural/social anthropology. Scholars like Nida (1954: 25), however, narrows down the discipline by dividing it into two main branches: physical/biological anthropology and cultural/social anthropology. Emphasising on the latter, which is the major focus of the present text, cultural anthropology is known as such in most American universities. Those universities with British orientation and culture call the same discipline social anthropology. In this book, the term "social anthropology" shall be used to refer to and, in fact, interchangeably with the term "anthropology" owing to the fact that the other broad subjects highlighted above [such as archaeology, biological/physical anthropology (i.e. palaeontology of primates, human genetics and evolution), and anthropological linguistics] are now studied as distinct and specialised fields in many universities across the world, and that these fields are somewhat beyond the limits of our immediate interest. In fact this book is about social anthropology.

While anthropology in general has the five aforementioned broad areas within its armpits, social anthropology also has many subfields. These include, but not limited to, the following: political anthropology, medical anthropology, environmental anthropology, anthropology of education, anthropology of development, Christian anthropology, urban anthropology, media anthropology, anthropology of science, and anthropology of experience/everyday life, among others.

The birth of social anthropology as an academic discipline

Though all societies across the world have always had mobile members who, in many cases, would always leave their societies of origin to live with members of other societies either temporarily or permanently, anthropology as an academic discipline has its origins in Europe. In the 18th and 19th

centuries in Europe and North America, the imperial nations developed colonies in distant parts of the world. While North Americans expanded west and south into the territories of Indians and Europeans expanded to Africa, it became clear to them that humanity across the world varied significantly especially in terms of culture and belief systems. This grand realisation generated curiosity among the elite and learned groups of the American and European societies. The need for a specific discipline that studies humanity across the world especially their cultures, ways of life, and belief systems proved a necessity. Social anthropology was therefore developed in Europe and the Americas out of necessity and with the major objective to study, understand, and record variations across cultures in the global world.

Yet, while the elite and learned group considered the understanding of other cultures an important adventure, the curiosity to understand strange and different cultures across societies especially in far off parts of the world was primarily generated and cultivated by early amateur social anthropologists, most of whom were medical doctors, Christian clerics, educated explorers, and geographers by profession (see Nida 1954). These amateur social anthropologists were initially concerned with understanding whether the differences between human cultures, skin colours, languages, among other such variations, were a result of genetic inheritance. They were also primarily concerned with understanding the relationship between the size of human brain and intelligence. It is, therefore, from the efforts and adventures of this pioneering research and curious quests that we now understand that appropriate answers to both of these questions is a no.

Nevertheless, it was not until the late 19th century that social anthropology became a separate and distinct academic discipline in Western Europe and northern American universities. It was also not until the 20th century that social anthropology as an academic discipline was introduced in some of the first universities on the African continent such as the University of Cape Town in South Africa.

While social anthropology continues to emphasise some of the things that amateur social anthropologists were curious to understand in the past, anthropology today asks fascinating and thought provoking questions about the nature and realities of things and humanity across human societies. It asks interesting questions and reveals avant-garde secrets and truths, through its quest for first-hand information, in all spheres of life – medical fraternity, education, politics, environmental science, and media etc. In fact, anthropology is one of the only disciplines that extend to other disciplines across the academy, what Paulin Hountondji (1983) encourages when he argues in view of African philosophers that:

> The responsibility of African philosophers (and all African scientists) extends far beyond the narrow limits of their discipline and that they cannot afford the luxury of self-satisfied apoliticism or the quiescent complacency about the established disorder unless they deny themselves as both philosophers and as people. In other words, theoretical liberation of philosophical discourse presupposes political liberation (p. 46).

Common assumptions in contemporary social anthropology

While social anthropology has many subfields such as political anthropology, anthropology of development, and environmental anthropology etc., one may, however, want to understand what makes all these subfields anthropological given their diversity. An answer to this is that all these subfields, and many others not mentioned here, assume the following in one way or another:

a) Human universalism

Human universalism entails that all people today are fully and equally human by nature. This implies that people from all societies around the world are equally complex, intelligent, dynamic, and interesting to study. We should, however, underscore that long ago, especially during the episodes of slavery and colonialism in Africa, human universalism did not hold as it does in contemporary social anthropology, that is, anthropology since the 1980s due to the Euro-centric thinking that undermined the intellectual capacities of other racial groups, especially the non-European ones. No wonder the Association for Anthropology in Southern Africa's Ethical Guidelines (AASA, 1987:2 (i) and (ii)) include the call to members to '... call attention to inequalities, cases of blatant injustice, violence and intrusion upon individual freedom ...' and also urged its members to declare themselves as totally opposed to the system of apartheid.

b) Cultural aspects are interrelated

The other common assumption in contemporary social anthropology is that every society has a culture that distinguishes itself from others. Differences between cultures are therefore tolerated and expected as normalcy while similarities are understood as coincidences. Yet, all the cultural aspects in a given culture, though might be distinct in a way, are interrelated such that understanding one cultural trait or institution requires one to know how the institution impacts and in turn is impacted by other institutions.

c)   Capacity to adapt

Adaptation entails the ability to acclimatise or adjust to given changes, whether natural or human-induced. Contemporary social anthropology as a scientific discipline assumes that all humanity across cultures of the global world has the ability to adapt to change in their environments. Social anthropologists in fact assume that people have flourished as a species because of their ability to adapt to their environments. This ability to adapt to changes in humanity is aided by our [humans] ability to think abstractly, acquire knowledge and create technology resulting in humans being unquestionably the most dominant and flourishing animal species on the land. This ability to adapt, thus, implies that human beings are the most skilled and complex of all beings on land, though might not be the strongest members of the animal kingdom considering that: we [humans] have relatively thin and soft skin. We are not the largest members of the animal kingdom in terms of body size. We can be killed and eaten by many other members of the animal kingdom such as lions, jackals and hyenas. We can't jump far and high. We can't fly. Neither are we the fastest members of the animal kingdom. The point however remains: that we [human beings] are far from all other animals such that to be equated to animals in any degree is not only a misnomer but in fact oprobrious.

d) Culture

Though too many definitions of culture have been conjured over the years, social anthropologists normally consider culture as the full range of learned behavioural patterns, knowledge, values and beliefs acquired by members of a given society over time. From this understanding, anthropologists assume that all humans have a culture which is not genetically inherent in them but learned through time. We, for example, learnt the culture we now consider ours from our parents or guardians who grew up with. This assumption in contemporary social anthropology is somehow different from what some Euro-American anthropologists and historians assumed especially in view of people of other continents such as Africa who they thought to be a people with no culture and philosophy. These scholars, for some time, corrupted the image of anthropology as a discipline to the extent that it became entrapped in power struggles and to the detriment of those it was intended to save, such as the powerless and voiceless. We will discuss this in detail in our next chapter. For now, let us tease out what social anthropology as an academic discipline is committed to study.

What does social anthropology study?

What does social anthropology as a discipline study? How does it study what it studies? These are normally questions that boggle the mind of anyone who hears or read anthropology for the first time. Given the diversity, dynamism, and wholesomeness of social anthropology as a discipline, these questions should not be treated lightly.

The fact remains that the field of social anthropology is so dynamic makes it possible to make important new discoveries on a daily basis especially in its subfields such as medical anthropology, urban anthropology, and environmental anthropology. The source of these new discoveries or 'fresh knowledge' is fieldwork and not laboratory experiments as those of the natural sciences. In fact, the laboratory of social anthropology is the field, and through fieldwork, social anthropologists acquire first-hand information about other societies and 'other beings'[2] (Mawere 2015). Social anthropology, through its powerful method of study, ethnography, enable social anthropologists to understand the nuances and complexities of humans, their behaviours, belief systems, and cultures and large. Social anthropology, thus, studies human societies in a holistic but nuanced manner that reveals finest details.

---

[2] We follow, one of the authors of this book, Professor Munyaradzi Mawere, who prefers using the term "other beings" to Bruno Latour (1987; 1993; 2005) and others' [i.e. Michel Callon 1986] "nonhuman" because for him there are some "creatures"/entities that are difficult to classify either as purely humans or nonhumans as they are part human and part nonhuman. In his 2015 publication, Mawere gives examples of Vampire and the Werewolf (see Jake Kosek 2010: 672), which he argues, are part human, part nonhuman becomings that result from the contagion of the battlefields. Basing on his ethnographic researches in the Norumedzo Communal Area in south-eastern Zimbabwe, Mawere also give many other examples of such entities as *vadzimu* (ancestors), *mhondoro* (lion spirits), and *njuzu* (mermaids/half fish half human creatures) that according to his interlocutors in the Norumedzo are not purely humans. Neither are they purely nonhumans, but are simply referred to by the locals (the interlocutors) as *zvisikwa zvaMwari* (other beings created by God). In this introductory chapter, we use the terms 'humans' and 'other beings', the latter to refer to all those entities that cannot be classified as humans both in part or in totality.

Insights from social anthropology

Social anthropology has, in the past, made (and continue to make) significant contributions to our knowledge especially that about ourselves and others, about our society and other societies. Through this contribution, those who study or have studied social anthropology have at least realised that social anthropology has the capacity to generate in people some important insights that help them understand themselves and others around them. Some of the insights generated from social anthropology are on:

a) People's orientations

Through social anthropological studies, one realises that life of a people is oriented in many different directions. Indigenous African people especially south of the Sahara traditionally glorify communalism, collective work, and mutual respect. Americans, on the other hand, have traditionally 'glorified strong individualism, the will to power, capitalism/accumulation of wealth, and the prestige which comes from being well known whether as a gangster like Al Capone, or as an actress like Marilyn Monroe' (Nida 1954: 53). As further reported by Nida, the Zuni culture is oriented around religious ceremonialism while the Shipibos of Peru glorify social integration and unity. Contrary to this, the Dobus of Melanesia would regard the Shipibo ideal as being a fool, for their life is oriented around treachery, magic, and anti-community social motives and extreme self-interest (Nida 1954).

b)   Pattern of human behaviour

Because anthropologists are acquainted with socio-cultural life in many societies, they often help people generate insights on patterns of human behaviour, able to correct and clarify beliefs and practices that could be generally accepted by their contemporaries. This means that through social anthropological insights and acquaintance with socio-cultural life in a variety of geographical settings, one realises that patterns in one society are normally interrelated. Eugene Nida (1954: 52) gives us a good example to illustrate this point. He notes that the fact that San Blas fishermen of the Indian society do not sell fish but will sell coconuts, does not reflect any lack of commercial interest in life. For Nida, these Indians are quite good businessmen, but fish are smoked and kept for fiestas, and a man's prestige and the acceptance of his daughter in society for puberty-rite festivals are partially dependent upon his ability to have enough fish to serve the guests. Coconuts are not, however, related to social activities such that they could be readily sold to anyone who offers an attractive price. Ember and Ember (1990: 2) also give another example from the United States. They note that when American educators discovered in the 1960s that black school children rarely drank milk, they assumed that lack of money or education was the cause. Evidence from anthropology, however, suggested a different explanation. Anthropologists had known for years that in many parts of the world where milking animals are kept, people do not drink fresh milk but sour it before they drink it or make it into cheese. Anthropologists such as Gail Harrison (1975) had also long provided another reason why people in other societies do not drink fresh milk. For Harrison, many people lack an enzyme, lactase, that is necessary for breaking down lactose, the sugar in milk. Such people cannot digest milk properly, and drinking it fresh will make them sick.

c) Conformity of human behaviour to a particular pattern

Social anthropology tells us that human behaviour is not something haphazard. It is something that always conforms to a particular pattern. We give an example of the VaDuma people of south-eastern Zimbabwe to illustrate our point. The fact that the VaDuma people, traditionally, do not cultivate (or even tamper with the environs) around the infamous Chingoma Falls do not reflect their any lack of agricultural interest in life. The VaDuma people are quite good farmers, but their preservation of the Chingoma Falls environs is largely based on their belief that the Falls are home to the much feared *Njuzu* (Mermaid/Water spirits) with the notorious history of kidnapping people especially those who temper with environs and resources around the Falls.

The uniqueness of social anthropology

As already alluded to, social anthropology is the study of human society in all its diversity: anthropology is 'the all-inclusive of human science' (Ember and Ember 1990: 3). It is the only academic discipline that seeks to understand all aspects of human life in its totality including the past and present socio-cultural processes and adaptations. But does social anthropology manage to do all this? Put differently, how does anthropology seek to understand all aspects of human life in its totality? Social anthropology does this by its rigorous focus on human variation in time and space, which in turn is possible given its [anthropology] practitioners' prolonged familiarity with the communities in which they participate in its daily life.

Also, given its broad focus and scope as well as its ability to deal with typical characteristics of particular populations, social anthropology is the most integrative discipline of all disciplines. It brings together scholarly work in the humanities, natural sciences, and social sciences; hence its interdisciplinary nature. Social anthropology, for example, deals with the social lives of people around the world including one's own society in terms of folklore, legal systems, political systems, economic systems, arts, and medical practices as well as interrelationships of these systems in relation to social change and environmental adaptation.

Besides, social anthropology is one of the most rigorous and illuminatory (if not the most) social science that shines on different societal and human problems to expose their multi-faceted dimensions. Franz Boas (1928), aptly explains the illuminatory role of social anthropology when he says: 'Anthropology illuminates the social processes of our time and may show us, if we are ready to listen to its teachings what to do and what to avoid' (p. 11). This is to say that anthropology has the capacity to effectively study human problems in their different contexts and throughout time as it reveals and illuminates problems through its continuous questioning of events, processes, assumptions, and phenomena in all spheres of human life. This way, anthropology can, as Gardener and Lewis (1996) argue 'can suggest alternative ways of seeing and thus step outside the discourse, both by supporting resistance to development and by working within the discourse to challenge and unpick its assumptions' (p. 25). John Bodley (2001: 11, emphasis original) also talking of the aptness of anthropology in responding to isolated problems notes that:

What is needed is perspective – a combination of detachment, a predilection for viewing the total picture in the widest spatial-temporal frame, and a clear recognition of the interrelatedness of social, cultural, biological and psychological factors. As an academic discipline, anthropology is uniquely qualified to offer just such an overview [...] In a sense, anthropology has been remarkably 'pre-adapted' to serve a sort of early-warning, equilibrium feedback function *due to its* holistic, cross-cultural, and evolutionary approaches.

These expositions should not be mistaken to mean that anthropology provides all answers we seek for our problems. The point is, anthropology is better placed to show us the nature of our problems, 'how we got where we are and suggest how we might get out' (Bodley 2001: 11), especially owing to the fact that 'anthropology is noted for the long periods its practitioners take to understand, multifacetedly and in detail, the communities or institutions they study' (Nyamnjoh 2006: 15).

Responsive relationship between anthropology and society

Anthropology is one of the closest disciplines to society: unlike many other disciplines, anthropology has a responsive relationship with society; hence a constructive discipline that one can ever think. Over the years, the responsive relationship between anthropology and the society in which anthropology as an academic discipline evolves, has often and cogently been shown by a number of anthropologists (cf. Asad, 1973; Hymes 1974; Scholte 1974, 1981; Barrett 1984). Hymes (1974), for example, encourages, anthropologists should '... ask of anthropology what they ask of themselves – responsiveness, critical awareness, ethical concern, human relevance, a clear connection between what is to be done and the interests of mankind' (p. 7).

As a discipline that seeks to understand humanity in totality, including the environment around him/her, anthropology is handy in all societies that need reconstruction, development and progression. Farris (1973) captures the responsive role of anthropology, perhaps better than anyone else before when he says:

> It is time that we lend 'the sanction of science' to eliminating oppression, and one (but only one) way of doing this is to make clear and attack the role of anthropology in creating, preserving, and implementing ideologies of oppression (p. 170).

Jansen van Rensburg writing of apartheid in South Africa in the early 90s, also sees the leading role that anthropology could and should assume to ensure reconciliation of races in post-apartheid South Africa. Rensburg (1994: 3), thus, emphasising and commenting on the responsive and reconstructive role of anthropology in South Africa had this to say:

> Since the abuse of anthropology in the colonial and apartheid eras, the responsive relationship between anthropology and society has been re-emphasised. In the reconstruction of South African society, therefore, anthropologists will not be allowed the luxury of evading their social responsibility. In their re-invention of anthropology as a humane science, and the reiteration of their commitment to accountability and relevance, these scientists ought to build their discipline upon the investigation of the major consequences of

differential power and inequality. This could be helpful in creating new forms of co-existence in South Africa.

As Rensburg commented above, there is no other science better placed than anthropology to negotiate social change and respond effectively to complex realities of phenomena such as oppression and apartheid in a manner that will foster reconciliation and 'conviviality *of the diverse races*' (Nyamnjoh 2004a, b; 2005; 2006; emphasis original), that is, the philosophy of races reaching out, encounter and exploring ways of enhancing or complementing themselves with the added possibilities of [positive] efficacy. Taking this argument further, Nyamnjoh (2006: 12) notes that:

> Anthropology and its methods have certainly served to foster imperialist appropriation of Africa, but as a discipline, it has undergone critical self-appraisal and re-orientation that should be instructive for communication research, other disciplines and fields of study interested in Africa, especially in the age of flexibilities and contestations of essentialisms.

Thus as Nyamnjoh tells us, anthropology as a discipline has since progressed from functionalist model of evolutionary change through binary oppositions of structuralism, to a clear understanding of social and cultural institutions as dynamic rather than static and stuck in space and time. Anthropology, thus, progresses and recreates itself with time as it responds to societal needs.

18

Chapter 2

Anthropology, Christianity, and the Colonial Project: A Search for a Humane Anthropology in Zimbabwe

"Anthropology illuminates the social processes of our times and may show us, if we are ready to listen to its teachings, what to do and what to avoid" (Boas 1928: 11).

Birth of a discipline: 'Morden' anthropology

'Modern' anthropology as we know it today developed as an academic discipline very late (in the 19th century). As Herbert Lewis (2014: 1) tells us, the origins of anthropology as an academic discipline can be dated from 1900 in the United States and 1927 in Great Britain, when the first doctorates were awarded to people trained in new canons of understanding and explanation and in the practice of extended fieldwork. Before this crop of anthropologists, anthropology was practiced by some exceptional individuals with sufficient curiosity to devote the effort and time to produce serious books about the ways of life of particular African peoples. It was, however, not until the late 1920s that the greatest increment to academic knowledge of African societies and cultures became significantly visible as more and more PhD students were trained in the British social anthropology of Bronislaw Malinowski[3] and A. R. Radcliffe-Brown.

---

[3] Bronislaw Kasper Malinowski was born in 1884 in Austria-Hungary (now Poland) and died in the United States of America in 1942. During his lifetime, Malinowski obtained a PhD in Philosophy from Jagiellonian

As an academic discipline, anthropology and in particular social anthropology, has been perceived as one of the most powerful of all social sciences in terms of its methods and approach to research (i.e. ethnography and participatory observation) and object of study (society and its inter- and intra-relationships). It is this potency associated with social anthropology that has witnessed the discipline placed at the centre of evangelists and those who assumed the role of civilising the world. In the next section we discuss in detail how social anthropology facilitated the European project of civilising the world through 'modern education' and Christianity.

University, another one in Physical Chemistry from the University of Leipzig before he obtained a 3rd PhD in Science from London School of Economics. Malinowski is commonly known as the Father of Social Anthropology and obviously one of the most important 20th century anthropologists given his notable contributions to the birth of the main research method in social anthropology (ethnography), an anthropological field method (where he coined the term participatory observation) he popularised when in 1914, he got the chance to travel to New Guinea accompanying anthropologist R. R. Marett. During this time, the World War 1 broke out and Malinowski being an Austrian (Polish) subject was an enemy of the British Commonwealth such that he was unable to travel back to England. The Austrian government nonetheless provided him with permission and funds to undertake ethnographic work within their territories and Malinowski chose to go to the Trobriand Islands in Melanasia (New Guinea) where he stayed for several years studying the indigenous cultures. When he returned to England after the war he published his main work *'Argonauts of Western Pacific'* in 1922 which established him as one of the most important anthropologists in Europe of that time. He later worked in several universities (in Britain and later America) as an Anthropologist, and he attracted a great number of students in Britain such as Evan-Pritchard, Meyer Fortes, Raymond Firth, and Edmund Leach. Malinowski is also known for his theory of functionalism where he emphasised that both social and cultural institutions serve basic needs, a perspective opposed to Radcliffe-Brown's structural functionalism that emphasised the ways in which social and cultural institutions function in relation to society as a whole.

Anthropology, Christianity, and civilisation in Africa

Anthropology is among one of the disciplines that alongside travel documents and the documentaries by early explorers of the likes of Marco Polo, Vasco da Gama, Bartholomew Dias, Christopher Columbers, and many others, was used to provide information for missionaries and later colonialists. The information that anthropologists provided was in fact used for different ends by different people from the global north. European missionaries, for example, used the information to understand cultures and languages of other societies so that their evangelical messages could be easily understood and received. This was necessary as without understanding the cultures and languages of their recipients, their evangelic message could have fallen on deaf ears: it could have never have been understood.

It is worth underlining that in southern Africa, European missionaries during the 19th and twentieth centuries played an outlandishly ambiguous role in the history, affairs and politics of the region. While on one hand, the missionaries had the genuine zeal and desire to serve humanity in what they considered as a civilising mission meant to bring about material and social fortunes to improve the qualitative aspects of human life, on the other hand, they perceived themselves as "moral superiors" with moral self-righteousness, which made them to hastily think that their moral values were far superior than those of the indigenous populations. This latter belief was largely influenced by the nefarious philosophies and mendacious researches of scholars such as David Hume, Immanuel Kant, Georg Hegel, Lucien Levy-Bruhl, Peter Winch, only to mention a few, who believed that Africa was "a dark continent" and its people "uncivilised." Hegel, in one of his writings, for example, obnoxiously had this to say of Africa and the [indigenous] people of Africa:

> The peculiarly African character is difficult to comprehend, for the very reason that in reference to it, we must quite give up the principle which naturally accompanies all *our* ideas-the category of Universality does not apply. In Negro life the characteristic point is the fact that consciousness has not yet attained to the realisation of any substantial objective existence-as for example, God, or Law-in which the interest of man's volition is involved and in which he realises his own being. This distinction between himself as an individual and the universality of his essential being, the African in the uniform, undeveloped oneness of his existence has not yet attained; so that the Knowledge of an absolute Being, an Other and a Higher than his individual self, is entirely wanting. The Negro, as already observed, exhibits the natural man in his completely wild and untamed state. We must lay aside all thought of reverence and morality-all that we call feeling-if we would rightly comprehend him; there is nothing harmonious with humanity to be found in this type of character. The copious and circumstantial accounts of Missionaries completely confirm this, and Mahommedanism appears to be the only thing which in any way brings the Negroes within the range of culture (Hegel Lectures, repub.1956: 93).

Hegel, thus, blatantly and unreasonably denied Africans rationality, knowledge and a sense of morality. In his widely celebrated Lectures, Hegel went on to "plant" the seed of division on Africa while at the same time attacking the dignity and humanity of the African people, thus:

At this point we leave Africa, not to mention it again. For it is no historical part of the World; it has no movement or development to exhibit. Historical movements in it – that is in its northern part – belong to the Asiatic or European World. Carthage displayed there an important transitionary phase of civilisation; but, *asisNahoenician* colony, it belongs to Asia. Egypt will be considered in reference to the passage of the human mind from its Eastern to its Western phase, but it does not belong to the African Spirit. What we properly understand by Africa, is the Unhistorical, Undeveloped Spirit, still involved in the conditions of mere nature, and which had to be presented here only as on the threshold of the World's History (Ibid: 99).

The French anthropologist-cum-philosopher, Lucien Levy-Bruhl (1910, 1922), also presented what he calls "savage states of mind" with reference to the African people. Basing on his ethnographic findings, Levy-Bruhl argues that the minds of the African people are so primitive and radically different from the Western logical ones. For this reason, he concludes that Africans are inferior to Europeans and their [Africans] minds are pre-logical and mystical, meaning that they are exclusively dominated by feelings. Many other racist celebrated scholars of the West such as Hume, Kant, and Mill, also unleashed uninvited barrage attacks on the African persona.

Equipped with and greatly influenced by this pejoratively bogus perception of Africans as "an uncivilised and inferior" race, the European missionaries sought to first, "throw" light on the religion of the African people by preaching Christianity to them. For the missionaries, if Africa was to ever "see light," it was necessary for her people to leave their "pagan" religion and follow the only authentic religion of the world, namely Christianity. This belief in European missionaries was buttressed by the fact that since the dawn of colonial rule, social/cultural anthropology in Africa, as the study of human cultures and peoples, largely viewed Africa from an outsider's perspective, without making an effort to reflect on the continent from inside. This way of viewing Africa has remained dominant even today where Africa's view of the world is normally articulated from the outside perspective, in most cases from the European viewpoint. It has been largely a result of the fact that when anthropology emerged as a discipline in the 1860s, Africa was never part of the world socio-economic system. This was in spite of the fact that it had now been four centuries earlier when contacts between Africa and the outside world were realised. This is what Michael Wood (2000) meant when he argues that the indigenous peoples were not considered to be human beings and that the colonisers were shaped by centuries of ethnocentrism and Christian monotheism, which espoused one truth, one time and version of reality. Realising the same, the indigenous Africans resisted the missionary initiative as they did not want to lose a grip on their indigenous epistemologies and traditional practices. It is on the basis of this resistance that Casalis wrote at Thaba Bosiu in Lesotho, in 1883 that:

> We said that, wishing to provide entirely for our own subsistence, we must have a site where we could build houses and cultivate the ground according to our own ideas and habits. Our buildings and plantations would also serve as a model for the Basutos, whom we regretted to see dwelling in huts, and living in a manner so precarious ad so little worthy of the intelligence with which they were gifted (SAHO 2016).

Second, the missionaries sought to help the indigenous Africans to improve on their agriculture by encouraging them to adopt what they called modern farming methods such as the use of synthetic fertilisers, irrigation and technology in general. Third, the missionaries sought to impose an alien morality and work ethos upon the indigenous Africans. Unfortunately, the missionaries did not realise that the imposition of their alien morality and work ethos greatly undermined the indigenous people's core cultural and social values as well as philosophy of life. For this reason, missionaries' initiatives met with serious resistance. Campbell (1885) corroborates this when he claim:

> Missionary stations are surrounded by moral atmospheres, or have a moral and civilising influence to a considerable distance around, beyond, it is extremely hazardous for white men to go, where they have strong objections... (SAHO 2016).

Colonialists, on the other hand, used the knowledge to understand the philosophies and cultures of other societies so that their penetration and conquest would be much easier.

While social anthropology has in the past been accredited with notches as a unifier of all humanities and sciences, it has in some parts of the world such as Africa, experienced a very sad history to the extent of some people doubting its adeptness and efficacy as a unifier of all other sciences and humanities. In the next section, we examine why many people in the sub-altern have, over the years, treated social anthropology with suspicion and scepticism.

Christianity and colonial projects in Africa: The Zimbabwean experience

Basing on the major reason that Catholicism and Protestantism were the religions of the European colonial powers engaged in colonial enterprise on a global scale, Christianity and colonialism are often closely related (cf. Page & Sonnenburg 2003). In fact, as Andrews (2010: 665) rightly notes:

> Christian missionaries were initially portrayed as visible saints, exemplars of ideal piety in a sea of persistent savagery. However, by the time colonial era drew to a close in the last half of the twentieth century, missionaries became viewed as ideological shock troops for colonial invasion whose zealotry blinded them.

It should be underscored that Christianity is often targeted by critics of colonialism chiefly because its tenets were used to justify most of the actions by colonialists. In line with this understanding, Falola (2001) argues that there were some missionaries who believed that the agenda of colonialism in Africa was similar to that of Christianity. To concretise his argument, Falola cite Jan H. Boer of the Sudan United Mission who had this to say:

> Colonialism is a form of imperialism based on a divine mandate and designed to bring liberation – spiritual, cultural, economic and political – by sharing the blessings of the Christ – inspired civilisation of the West with a people suffering under satanic oppression, ignorance and disease, effected by a combination of political, economic and religious forces that

cooperate under a regime seeking the benefit of both ruler and ruled (Ibid: 33).

Similarly, Andrews (2010) though expounds on Falola by offering two perspectives on the way Christian missionaries have been viewed over the years, reverberates with Falola's assertion above as he avers:

Historians have traditionally looked at Christian missionaries in one of two ways. The first church historians to catalogue missionary history provided hagiographic descriptions of their trials, successes, and sometimes even martyrdom. Missionaries were, thus, visible saints, exemplars of ideal piety in a sea of persistent savagery. However, by the middle of the twentieth century, an era marked by civil rights movements, anti-colonialism, and growing secularisation, missionaries were viewed quite differently. Instead of godly martyrs, historians now described missionaries as arrogant and rapacious imperialists. Christianity became not a saving grace but a monolithic and aggressive force that missionaries imposed upon defiant natives. Indeed, missionaries were now understood as important agents in the ever-expanding nation-state, or ideological shock troops for colonial invasion whose zealotry blinded them.

Thus, many critical historians and theorists of colonialism view Christian missions as nothing but an enterprise of Western cultural and religious imperialism.

We however, note in this book that although some early missionaries such as Robert Moffat acted as forerunners of colonialism in some parts of Africa such as Zimbabwe, we should not paint all missionaries with one brush, as a people who advanced the interests of colonialism and imperialism. In fact, there were some missionaries who were sympathetic of the indigenous Africans to the extent that they supported the guerrilla struggle against European colonialism. In Zimbabwe, for example, sections of the Catholic Church criticised the Ian Smith regime for its aggressive and oppressive treatment of the African people. The church even went a step further to chronicle some of the atrocities by the Ian Smith regime and also admitted to assisting guerrillas, though sometimes they did this willingly and at other times under duress. Bishop Donald Lamont of Umtali (now Mutare) is worth mentioning as a case of reference for the Catholic sections that sympathised with the African people during their struggle for independence (cf. Siamonga 2016). Another good example in Rhodesia (now Zimbabwe) was also Missionary Guy Clutton-Brock, who was post-humously declared a national hero for his active role in standing against the oppression of the Zimbabwean people, and building schools and hospitals in the country. Coming back to Bishop Lamont, it is known that he experienced a protracted trial for his role as a sympathiser and supporter of the guerrillas to the extent that he was later on deprived of his citizenship as a Rhodesian and deported by the then stickler Minister of Law and Order, Hillary Squires. In a statement before Lamont's deportation, Squires had this to say:

> I have had more than enough of the intellectual arrogance of his beliefs, of his continued denigration of what the government has ever done, (attacking innocent civilians and fighting guerrillas) while continuing to enjoy the benefit and, most especially, the hypocrisy of his selective conscience of supporting the struggle (Ibid).

Thus, although some Christian churches in the country then, such as the Anglican condemned the guerrillas' struggle against colonialism to the extent of labelling them as "terrorists," missionaries like Lamont and Clutton-Brock remained outspoken and an ardent supporter of the rise of African nationalism.

What remains suspicious in the link between colonialism and Christianity, however, is the fact that the colonial period facilitated the coming in of a great number of missionaries to spread the gospel to the people of Africa whose ethnic frontiers were torn into pieces by the European rule.

With its emphasis on participatory observation, anthropology has, for a long time, acted as a source for many seekers of knowledge of world societies. As a primary source of knowledge about the African peoples, cultures and societies, anthropology's active role predates the colonial era on the continent [Africa]. Having recognised the strength of anthropology as the only social science that can offer a holistic picture of a people and most credible information about human societies, anthropology has been used by some colonial architects as a rich source of information about the African peoples and other such societies. It is for this major reason that when Cecil John Rhodes sent his delegate to entice King Lobengula of Matabeleland into signing a treaty with the British South African Company (BSAC), he made sure to include among Charles Rudd and company (Rochford Maguire), Robert Moffat and Francis Thomson who were missionary and conversant and fluent in Ndebele respectively, and who through Lotshe "tricked" Lobengula to sign the Rudd Concession. The emergence of early missionaries is, thus, critical in understanding the role that anthropology played in paving way for both Christianity and colonialism.

After having been unrecognised as part of the world system for nearly five centuries, Africa is realised as part of the world economic system again in the nineteenth century. This recognition started with the trans-Atlantic slave trade which led to the creation of European stations on the African coast for the recruitment of human capital – slaves – from the continent. Despite the abolition of slavery in most of the world, by the late 19th century, European empires competed for position and access to the human and material resources of Africa. This led to the treaty of Berlin, in 1878, which granted any "civilised state" to occupy the coastal African region, the right to claim the hinterland (cf. Graniage 1969). The 1878 Berlin treaty ultimately led to the 1884 Berlin Conference which culminated into "the scramble for Africa", with enormous outpouring of explorers, missionaries, hunter and travellers who would shape the future of anthropological work on the continent. It emerged during the Conference that Africa had become an integral part of the world's economic system, not only as a supplier of human capital, but that of natural resources. After the Berlin Conference, the European imperialists of Europe used their anthropological knowledge of the continent of Africa to penetrate and infiltrate African societies. It is this active role of anthropology as a feeder of information about the cultures, philosophies and languages resulted in its history being tainted and its very nature characterised as a mixed bag, especially during the nineteenth and twentieth centuries.

Cracks in the facades of colonial anthropology: A search for a humane anthropology

It is no secret that anthropology in Africa since the demise of colonial administration in Africa has been viewed with a negative eye by both critical scholars on Africa and African governments. Indeed throughout the 1960s to the present, many African governments demonstrated their scepticism and suspicion of the discipline, anthropology, given the role it played before and during colonialism on the continent.

There was need for them to take action if anthropology as discipline was to survive. This scepticism and suspicion led to the establishment of the Journal: *Présence Africaine* in the 1940s as a reaction among African and African-American intellectuals against what they saw as a persistent failure to recognise adequately Africa's role in world history. This reaction, mainly by scholars and African politicians, later developed into what came to be known as Pan-Africanism through initiatives by Kwame Nkrumah and others. This movement – PanAfricanism – was to be a formidable force against colonialism and neocolonialism on many of Africa's early post-colonial leaders and intellectuals.

It should be underlined that English-speaking anthropologists dominated anthropology during the colonial period of the African continent, perhaps simply because of their embracement of the philosophical doctrine of empiricism, which fostered besides respecting observation also paid greater respect for local culture. It is mainly for this major reason that we see English-speaking anthropologists serving colonial administrators whose mandate was to rule through local personnel such as chiefs and headmen. This gave anthropologists the opportunity to assert themselves more creatively both on the intellectual front and in the political discourse of the European colonies. This positioning of anthropologists saw the discipline emerging in the university system in Great Britain in 1925, together with the creation of a state-sponsored research institute, the *International Institute of African Languages and Culture* (IIALC). This institute, which was later known as the *International African Institute* or (IAI) had as one of its main objective, to study and gather large amounts of ethnographic data on Africa, which was used both properly and abusively by the colonialists. This role, that anthropology assumed, further consolidated the discipline during the colonial era.

By 1928, the *International Institute of African Languages and Culture* had established the Journal: *The African Survey* in 1928, under the Editorship of Lord Hailey. This journal inspired important monographs on African politics such as Meyer Fortes's (1940) edited volume: *African Political Systems* and Daryll Forde's 1954 volume on cosmology and religion with the title: *African Worlds*, as well as John Middleton, David Tait, and Laura Bohannan's 1958 edited volume: *Tribes Without Rulers*. The journal also inspired other works by Radcliffe-Brown and Daryll Forde's (1956) *African Systems of Kinships and Marriage*, Levi-Strauss's (1966) Anthropology: Its Achievements and Future, as well as studies on witchcraft such as Middleton and Winter's (1963) *Witchcraft and Sorcery in East Africa*. Recent English-speaking anthropological figures inspired by the same journal include Evans-Pritchard, Levi-Strauss, Victor Turner, Audrey Richards, and Mary Douglas. All these anthropologists and anthropological works captured, in varying ways, the imaginations and philosophies of indigenous Africans, such that the demand of anthropology during the colonial era became so immense than almost none of the other social sciences of the time. Even emerging African scholars were soon to join the discipline in the colonialist's attempt to understand the African societies even more comprehensibly. Kofi Busia of Ghana, Archie Mafeje of South Africa, Cheikh Anta Diop of Senegal, and Jomo Kenyatta of Kenya, all committed themselves to anthropology in very serious ways. Kenyatta, for example, was one of the earliest African intellectuals to study, in the 1930s, under Malinowski, culminating in his infamous 1938 publication: *Facing Mount Kenya*. Mafeje (1963; 1966; 1969; 1970; 1971a; 1971b; 1975; 1976a; 1976b; 1977; 1978) after his training at the University of Cape Town, under the mentorship of Monica Wilson, became one of the most critical and prolific Africanist anthropologist of both the colonial and post-colonial Africa.

Elsewhere, in Africa, the development of anthropology was largely through the work of two key government sponsored institutes: *Institut Francaise pour l'Afrique Noire* (IFAN) and *Organisation de Recherche Scientifique et Technique d'Outre Mer* (ORSTOM). IFAN was established by the French government to principally compare and document the customs and traditions of African "tribal groups." On the other hand, ORSTOM, was established to conduct more comprehensive studies in all French colonies, including those in Africa. Its researches mainly focused on cultural, social, human, health, mineral, and geological studies, all through ethnographic field trips.

Yet, despite feeding and largely dependent on anthropological studies for the success of the colonial enterprise, the colonial governments remained suspicious of anthropology as a discipline. They seemed aware of the potential of anthropology to serve a double role. Also, due to intense pressure from the rising nationalism in Africa,

Africanist anthropologists from the West withdrew from studies on the continent during the 1960s so as to avoid blackmailing. They feared being labelled as prominent advocators of the colonial cause in Africa, which none of them seemed to support. This fear largely came amidst Western anthropologists such as Levi-Bruhl's nefarious claims and pejorative labelling of the African people. Levi-Bruhl, following philosophers such as Hegel, Kant, Wittgenstein, Hume, Mill and others in advancing the political and colonial project of Europe, identified Africans as the "primitive" or "savages". He popularised the idea that the African race was in all respects inferior to the European race.

Consequently, with the retreat of Africanist anthropologists and the vitriolic attack of Africa by anthropologists such as Levi-Bruhl, Peter Winch and Horton in the 1960s, there was, in the 20th century, the fear for the demise and the need to renew the discipline of anthropology in view of allegations and perceptions that yielded in the 1960s when independence for Africa appeared imminent preoccupied anthropologists. This fear, thus, was promulgated largely as a result of the widely debated prevailing belief about Africans as was popularised by works of anthropologists and philosophers of the like of Levi-Bruhl and his cabal. Peter Winch (1964), for example, had taken position along with Levi-Bruhl and their predecessor, Wittgenstein, to reason was convolutedly linked to language and culture, with the "higher" culture of Europe being associated with higher reason as opposed to that of the "low" cultures of Africa. Horton (1967) had also described African societies as "unscientific" and "closed" as opposed to the "open" and "scientific" societies of Europe.

As is known, at independence, each new nation-state had to create its own institutions of higher learning such as universities and colleges, but with a curriculum based on that of the European universities and colleges. The creation of institutions of higher learning was premised on the widely held belief that the transfer of scientific knowledge was critical for national development. Socio-economic-related international donors and non-governmental organisations supported such initiatives by African governments for majority of them also believed that education was the only gateway to success and development of the newly independent African states. Most of these organisations (donor funders and NGOs), thus, rallied around the national governments' objective to produce trained and skilled manpower, to work in both the government and the private institutions. African people with overseas training were recruited in many institutions of higher learning to teach alongside, and gradually replace, expatriates. Throughout the 1960s and 1970s, when many African countries emerged independent, the returning graduates from overseas were guaranteed high salaries, decent houses, and vehicles, as a way of luring them back home.

Curriculum-wise, very little attention was paid to the study of African cultures in higher institutions of learning as the main focus was on the arts. While many of the Africanists who emerged as leaders at Africa's independence claimed African roots for their Marxist and socialist political ideology, very few of them relied on anthropology to provide the basis for such an ideology. Many of these leaders spoke of the need to embrace African culture without meshing their words with practice. As Sawadogo (1995) reveals, two UNESCO Conferences (one in Monrovia in 1979 and another in Yaoundé in 1984) called for the teaching of African languages and cultures, but this simply never happened in most countries. Anthropology could have provided the material for such a curriculum, but the discipline was not taken seriously, carrying the stigma, as it did, of its ties to the colonial past. Instead, many African nationalist governments practically turned to the popular modernisation theory, which according to many theorists, had the potential to transform the fortunes of Africa into what was hoped to be an economic supremacy. Regrettably, basing on their own experiences during the colonial period, nationalist governments continued to regard anthropology as a tool of colonial subjugation and as a discipline of no relevance for the new and modernising Africa (Nkwi 2000; 1989; 1998a; 1998b). This had a setback on the development and promotion of anthropology as a university discipline. The setback was coupled with the fact that at independence African and Africanist anthropologists found it difficult to openly practice their profession due to the negativities associated with anthropology. As Crossman and Devisch (1999) observed, at Makerere University in Kampala, for example, the British had, during the colonial period, established the Institute of Cultural Anthropology (ICA) to promote ethnographic research in the country and beyond, but this once flourishing institute disappeared into the sociology department after independence. The same happened in many other universities in Africa such as the University of Zimbabwe and the University of Zambia, where the once flourishing Anthropology Departments were swallowed by sociology. The question remains: "What anthropology should have done to assume a humane face? Or: With its efficacy, as demonstrated during colonialism, why anthropology failed to deconstruct itself and firmly re-establish itself as a powerful discipline?"

Crossman and Devisch (Ibid) answer this question so meticulously. They argue that the problem that faced anthropology in independent Africa is that its deconstructionist paradigms emanated from the global north instead of emanating from with Africa herself. This made African governments' negative beliefs on anthropology unabated. African governments continued viewing anthropology as a colonial discipline with the major objective of reaffirming colonialism on the continent. This made it more difficult of anthropology practitioners to deconstruct and reconstruct the discipline in such a way that would erase all the suspicion around it. It is partly for this reason and the vitriolic attacks that many times the discipline of anthropology has, since the independence of Africa, been declared dead by distinguished anthropologists and leaders in the field such as Levi- Strauss, Jacque Maquet, James Hooker, Peter Worsley, and Rodney Needham, among others. To be more precise, in 1966 all of a sudden Levi-Strauss, in an article, "Anthropology: Its Achievements and Future," expressed appreciation of the growing hostility in developing countries towards anthropology as a result of the role that the discipline played during colonialism. He reasoned that for anthropology to be ever viewed as legitimate in formerly colonised countries, it must undergo a revolutionary metamorphosis and disengage itself from the colonial system and all its institutions. He further argues that anthropology must become a study of society from the inside, breaking down into a number of disciplines, if at all the discipline is to survive in this changing world. In other words, there was need, Levi-Strauss' view, for anthropology to allow itself to perish in order to be born again in a new costume. Similarly, in a paper entitled simply: "The End of Anthropology" (1968), Peter Worsley (1966) expressed his fears on the future of anthropology. Worsley's fears were however not a result of his realisation of anthropology's colonial parentage. It was rather premised on anthropology's perpetual hanging on theoretical parochialism and fixation about the "primitive" world whose emergent relations in postcolonial period were fast changing. For this reason, Worsley reasoned for the need to adopt a new universalism outside the old imperial frame, if ever anthropology was to survive. In the same year, Kathleen Gough (1968) shocked many anthropologists in the field by outrightly declaring anthropology "the child of Western imperialism". Yet remaining clinging on the discipline, Gough sought to radicalise anthropology by suggesting that it ceases to interpret the non-western world from the standpoint of the values of Western capitalist society. She challenged anthropologists to first shake off the colonial chains in their hands and free themselves from the limitations imposed on them by their own Western orientations. Two years later, the British anthropologist, Rodney Needham (1970) criticised anthropology for lacking a comprehensive theoretical coherence and rigour. This lack of theoretical coherence and rigour, for Needham, had the potential, over time, to send the discipline of anthropology to the graves. As recent as 1991, Ife Amadiume, an African sociologist, recommended the need to abolish anthropology and turning it into "African social history and sociology of history" (Mafeje, 1997:22).

Nevertheless, defending the face of anthropology, Raymond Firth (1972), a leading British anthropologist, denied absolutely that anthropologists were indifferent to the fate of the colonised. Contrary to the likes of Worsley (1966) and Gough, Firth claimed that anthropologists sought to gain respect for the people they studied and not to subjugate or promote their subjugation in any way. He further argued against Firth claiming that anthropology is not the bastard of imperialism, but the legitimate child of the Enlightenment.

The implication of this whole criticism meant that there was need to liberate anthropology in Africa if the legitimacy of the discipline was to be anything worth celebrating. This anticipatory deconstruction and reconstruction (or rebirth) of the anthropology was the only surest way to guarantee the survival and continued celebration of the discipline in Africa. We argue in this book that, perhaps with the exception of critical African anthropologists such as Mafeje (1975; 1976b; 1977; 2001) and Magubane (1971), the transformation of anthropology in Africa remained exclusively a process to be realised by the global north. Other African anthropologists on the continent such as Gordon Chavunduka remained prominent, but not in the process of deconstructing anthropology on the continent. A survey of his anthropological works after independence, shows that while he practiced anthropology upto the time of his death, he didn't preoccupy himself with the urgent need of deconstructing anthropology in Africa in order to make it more viable and relevant on the continent. His focus continued directed more on witchcraft and medicine to the expense of ensuring the welfare, relevance and viability of the discipline as a whole.

While in countries like South Africa, anthropology continued to function as a formal discipline in many universities such as the universities of Cape Town (UCT), Witwatersrand University, Rhodes University, Stellenbosch University, University of Pretoria, Port Elizabeth University, and University of Natal, these institutions did not provide little support to anthropology departments of smaller universities in the country and beyond. Besides, we see the likes of Kofi

Busia, the Ghanaian who is one of the Africanists to study anthropology, establishing the Department of Sociology, instead of Anthropology, at the University of Ghana-Legon. He, however, later on head the department of anthropology at Leiden University in the Netherlands. Other Africanists like Jomo Kenyatta, a student of Malinowski, had to use his anthropological skills to construct the *Mau Mau* Movement to lead the struggle against the European rule in Kenya. Kenyatta, thus, though continuing using anthropology in his life, he abandoned the discipline as a practitioner as he finds home in politics. On the same note, other leading African anthropologists like Adam Kuper, John Comaroff, and Archie Mafeje could be seen leaving their countries in search of more conducive environments to seriously practice their anthropology.

The failure of pioneering African anthropologists to deconstruct and resuscitate the discipline of anthropology resulted in anthropology taking cover within African Studies programs especially since the 1970s and 1980s as the criticism again the discipline intensified. Centres and institutes of African Studies emerged in many countries across Africa and beyond, with anthropology and ethnography being taught and practiced. Besides, anthropology has increasing been labelled as one of the branches of sociology and was taught within the promising departments of sociology in many African universities. In Zimbabwean universities, for example, anthropology to date remains attached to the discipline of sociology, with the latter tending to overshadow the former. At the University of Zimbabwe and Great Zimbabwe University, anthropology is housed under the department of sociology. At both universities, more sociological courses are taught as compared to anthropology. In other universities, both state and private, in the country such Midlands State University (MSU), Africa University (AU), Solusi University (SU), Chinhoyi University of Technology (CUT), National University of Science and Technology (NUST), Women's University (WU), Bindura University of Science Education (BUSE), and Zimbabwe Ezekiel Guti University (ZEGU), anthropology as a discipline is not even included in the curriculum. All this is a clear testimony that anthropology is fast losing followers in the country, hence the need to resuscitate the discipline and restate its relevance in contemporary society. As Mafeje (2001) tells us, the lack of deconstruction efforts of the discipline of anthropology by African practitioners could be attributed to such factors as the intellectual hegemony of the North, the intellectual immaturity of African anthropologists or the static conception of what anthropology was about.

Trapped between the pufferies of the desire to break away with the colonialist past and that of attaining progress, the practice of the discipline of anthropology in Africa, however, remains at its lowest ebb. It remains threatened with the risk of disappearing from the scene and for good, in many African universities. With this realisation, many questions arise: What then, should anthropology do to survive the scourge? Who should resuscitate the discipline from its imminent eternal death? What does the death of anthropology mean to practitioners in the field? What is the implication of the death of anthropology to both African governments and people?

Briefly, we argue in view of the questions highlighted above and the status of the anthropology on the continent that there is need for African anthropologists to rethink their roles as old banana trees that should leave suckers behind. We discuss more on this in chapter three.

Chapter 3

Anthropology, Politics and Recognition: A Disciplinary Struggle

Introduction

Although African cultures and traditions have historically been condemned for resistance to colonially inspired change [that was alluringly but misleadingly called modernity], the contemporary resistance by academics and academies to the (re-)introduction of anthropology represents reactionary logics that would have surprised many native commissioners. Contemporary academies and academics have become front liners in resisting change that seeks to bring in contemporary variants of anthropology that are equipped with cutting edge decolonial research that takes into bona fide account the cultural, traditional, religious, environmental, political, epistemic, and economic experiences of the African people. Since, recently, Euro-modernist projects including Euro-Enlightenment have become troubled by critics who charge that they constituted foundational projects in the colonisation, imperial dispossessions and domination of African people, academies and academics in Africa need to recognise that the tools used by imperialists were much broader than anthropology as a discipline. To remain beholden to the Euro-modernist and Euro-enlightenment projects, which equally served as foundations for the colonisation of Africans, while at the same time rejecting anthropology [on the premise that it was used by colonists], would be to run into deep paradoxical boxes. The epistemic and ontological changes [or shifts] that are currently knocking at the "doors" of African academies and academics largely go unnoticed by those that have been "drinking" at the shrines of Euro-modernity and Euro-enlightenment for centuries: preferring as they often do to summarily dismiss anything that focuses on understanding and privileging African cultures, economies, polities, traditions, religions and environments.

Politics of resistance and the question of disciplinary nativism

Anthropology has often been criticised for being a handmaiden of colonialism, particularly because colonial native commissioners relied on the discipline to understand cultures and relational ontologies of "natives" before colonising them. However, those that dismiss anthropology from the community of disciplines in the academies hardly notice that they are engaging, in the contemporary era, in the logic of [disciplinary] nativism in which anthropology as a discipline suffers [disciplinary] apartheid within the postcolonial academies. Academies suffering disciplinary nativism and disciplinary apartheid merely replicate the logics of colonists and native commissioners who were charged with keeping boundaries between citizens and subjects or between White colonists and Black Africans that were subjugated. Thus, the exclusionary nature of academic spaces is premised on logics of apartheid but in a disciplinary sense. The nativism over which native commissioners used to preside has been transposed to academies which have de facto commissioned [disciplinary] native commissioners who take pleasure in policing disciplinary borders for purposes of excluding some. In many African academies; mention African culture, indigenous knowledge, African traditions and so on, and this would frighten some academics who have imbibed colonial gospels about the impurities of Africa cultures, traditions, indigenous knowledge and so on. In other words, those including anthropologists who study African cultures, economies, polities and knowledge systems are often deemed to threaten the purity of academies that are soaked in Euro-enlightenment and Euro-modernist projects that constitute and treat the Africans as "others" including on their own continent.

The contemporary resistance to anthropology in African academies should not be simplistically understood in terms of the discipline's association with colonialism because all disciplines including science were imbricated in the colonial project. Rather, the contemporary resistance to the discipline should be understood in terms of the continuation of the otherisation of Africans whose epistemologies are excluded from academies, by virtue of exclusion of a discipline that is privileged to study their epistemologies. In this sense, it is otherisation by means of excluding disciplines most relevant to understanding Africans and their knowledge systems. But otherisation also appears in the form of including entailing inclusion merely as an appendage to the mainstream other. In this sense, anthropology is excluded from many academies in Africa and when it is included, it appears merely as an appendage of another mainstreamed discipline such as sociology, development studies or African studies. So much like in the colonial era when an African could only be understood in terms of the colonially mainstreamed European beings, anthropology is understood and interpreted as an appendage of the mainstreamed disciplinary others. This is disciplinary colonialism that has implications for other forms of coloniality.

It is cause for wonder that in a world that makes so much noise about mainstreaming the previously marginalised, very little if any efforts are made to mainstream postcolonial anthropology including the epistemologies and cultures of those that it studies. A lot of noise is often made about the need for inclusion and inclusivism, yet in many academies there is spirited resistance to the inclusion of disciplines such as postcolonial anthropology that assist in understanding Africans and in designing projects that free them from ongoing coloniality. One wonders about the sincerity of discourses on mainstreaming and on including Africans in [global] development, policy and other projects: in a context where the epistemologies, perspectives, cultures and traditions of the Africans are actively resisted and doomed to the dustbins, the logics of inclusion are defeated. Although it may be argued that Africans are included and mainstreamed, as individuals and so without their cultures, epistemologies and traditions; one wonders whether they remain Africans if shorn of their cultures, epistemologies and traditions (Nhemachena, 2016a). In other words, one wonders about what is being mainstreamed if the epistemologies of the subalterns are neglected and even actively resisted in the academies that claim to be vanguards of inclusivism and bearers of light on the continent.

In thinking through the exclusion of and resistance to anthropology as a discipline in African universities, it is necessary to notice that the exclusion of the discipline by extension implies the exclusion of African cultural and epistemic desiderata. Thus, it is Africans and academics who have been cultured by colonialism to run away from their own cultural shadows that would prefer to be mainstreamed after being carefully trimmed of their cultures, contexts and traditions (Nhemachena, 2016a; Fanon, 1963). In such a scenario, anthropology becomes moribund and any students of the discipline risk being asked by sceptics about its relevance and what they will do or benefit from studying the discipline. In other words, while Nhemachena, (2016b) notes that even in the United Kingdom and the rest of Europe they have retained their Queens and Kings and hence their traditions and cultures, in Africa academies and academics [aided by some civil society organisations that condemn African cultures and traditions] train citizens to run away from their traditions and cultures and, by extension, from disciplines like anthropology that are deemed to be too close to African traditions and cultures.

From the experience that we have had in the academies, some academics, even in cognate disciplines like sociology, deride anthropology as the study of subcultures. While there may be necessity to applaud their courage to attempt to define a discipline that they have not studied, to consider anthropology to be a discipline that merely focuses on studying subcultures is to be utterly lost in one's disciplinary arrogance. African cultures and epistemologies, which are the subjects of anthropology, cannot conceivably be subcultures on the African continent. Consequently, academies and academics that trivialise anthropology and by extension the subject of African culture in fact trivialise the majority of citizens of the African continent.

Ignorant that even the disciplines like sociology, psychology, law and so on were similarly originated to deal with social, psychological and legal problems, and thus with the marginalised including the poor, some academics erroneously consider anthropology as the only discipline that studies the marginalised, that is, subcultures. Furthermore, they fail to notice that anthropology is not merely about studying the marginalised and subcultures but it also involves what is called studying up in which researches about the powerful and influential are conducted. Even during the colonial era, some anthropologists, while studying Africans, also studied and wrote about the colonial settlers (see for example, Nida 1954). So, to argue and summarily dismiss anthropology as the study of subcultures is to manifest gargantuan ignorance about the thrust of anthropology as a discipline as well as about its utility in assisting in decolonising contemporary Africa. The immense ignorance about the utility of and thrust of the discipline of anthropology even by academics in cognate disciplines speaks to Nhemachena's (2016b) argument that many academies are wittingly or unwittingly involved in the social and epistemic production of ignorance that then masquerades as knowledge. How one can criticise and dismiss anthropology and the attendant memories of native commissioners while at the same time acting as a disciplinary [academic] native commissioner baffles progressive minds.

Some academics in Africa have even gone to the extent of dismissing Anthropology and the attendant privileging of African cultures and traditions as nativism, as essentialism of Africans and hence as backward. Thus, to study African cultures and traditions is to risk being associated with the backward, atavistic and barbaric. In this sense, those that consider anthropology to be a study of atavism, backwardness and so on, are in fact labouring under colonial constructions of [linear] time. In other words, they use colonial constructions of time to dismiss anthropology as a colonial discipline.

Little attention is paid to the fact that the same academics have become [chief disciplinary] native commissioners albeit with global [colonial] mandates to mediate between Africa and the West. The only difference is that while some native commissioners tolerated some African cultures and traditions to the extent that they could be employed to further the colonial projects, African postcolonial "native" commissioners dismiss African traditions, cultures and epistemologies even if these can help their fellow Africans to resist encroachments by global coloniality. In other words, while it appears that with the demise of formal colonialism colonial native commissioners were decommissioned, the reality is that logics of colonial native commissioning were simply transposed to academies and academics that now mediate between global coloniality and African realities. The only difference is that contemporary native commissioners perform worse than colonial native commissioners because they have chosen to completely banish anthropology from their service.

While dismissing anthropology as a discipline, African academics have often paradoxically mediated for global transnational corporations' exploitation of African indigenous knowledge. Similarly, while rejecting anthropology as a colonial discipline, some academics [irrespective of discipline] have mediated between global institutions and corporations that trawl and exploit, and dispossess [contemporary] Africans. In this sense, while anthropology can be helpful in retracing colonial distortions and destruction of African systems, the discipline is often uncritically and summarily dismissed and rejected. Sadly, while the academies reject anthropology as a colonial discipline they continue on the antecedent colonial trajectory. Jettisoning the discipline of anthropology is not necessarily all that is required to jettison [neo-]colonialism.

If, as is the case, some Africans who supported and assisted the colonial projects were not rejected but accepted back into their postcolonial communities [even if with some purification rituals], it would not make much sense rejecting a discipline such as anthropology on the premise that it was used during the colonial era. Colonists used guns, machetes, bayonettes, aircraft and ammunition which Africans cannot and have not rejected. What is needed is simply to purify the disciplines and then use them to promote contemporary decolonial projects instead. Purification of the discipline of anthropology would involve not merely continued research but also crafting theories from Africa using African data (Nhemachena *et al*, 2016). It would involve ensuring that African data and African beings are not used for nefarious global colonial projects. Purification of the discipline would involve the employment of the discipline to ensure African epistemologies are safeguarded and used for the benefit of the continent and not for the benefit of transnational corporations and Western (or generally global north) institutions. It would also ensure that African epistemologies are not distorted by researchers who come to the continent to research and then write about Africans in ways that perpetuate the caricaturing of their ways of life.

While there are benefits of including anthropology as a discipline in the African academies, the challenge is that global coloniality will likely not be disposed to invest in anthropological research that genuinely helps Africans resist the same global coloniality. The danger is that global coloniality, just like colonialism, will only invest in types of anthropological researches that perpetuate global coloniality and the attendant profiteering by the global transnational corporations that continue to dispossess and exploit the African people. Thus, the resuscitation of the discipline of anthropology would likely be premised on its continued trajectory as a global (neo-)colonial discipline if it is funded by the same organisations and corporations that funded it during the colonial era. It would be naïve to think that the old colonial and imperial funders would change their spots and sincerely fund the resurgence of the discipline on a genuinely new trajectory meant to bring about genuine decolonisation in the global south. Colonialism and empire have been located in the labyrinth of Western capitalism and it is sadly the same capitalism that runs the world and decides which disciplines and researches to fund and invest in.

As a discipline that mediates the Euro-modern and the African cultural realms, anthropology promises liberation to Africans but it also threatens them with doom and gloom if African anthropologists are not vigilant about the ulterior motives of funders. Doom and gloom come in when anthropology is funded by global elites who often "generously" sponsor researches for purposes of legitimating their global governance. Thus, disciplinary researches are often useful for global elites as they can be tools to generate the consent of Africans to be governed by those global elites that continue to dispossess and exploit the impoverished. The [contemporary] discourses hinted above about the inclusion of Africans and their cultures and epistemologies in the global realms would require anthropologists to mediate the processes of global inclusion but the critical question is inclusion in what sense and as what or in what form? In much anthropological literature, it is for instance, hardly mentioned that since the enslavement era through to the colonial one, Africans have been included but as cannon fodder for global and imperial projects. Similarly, African resources, epistemologies, cultures, polities and societies have been included in the imperial and colonial projects but as fodder for imperial projects.

To reject the discipline of anthropology on the basis that it was used by colonialist to colonise Africans would not sustain critical analysis in that postcolonial Africa has reconciled with the colonist at independence. Thus, to reconcile with the former colonists but fail to reconcile with the disciplines that they used to colonise others would not be intellectually sound and appealing. Rejecting the discipline of Anthropology on account of it having served as the handmaiden of colonialism would be to accept political reconciliation but fail to concede reconciliation at a disciplinary and epistemic level. So, if Anthropology as a discipline was the [disciplinary] maid of colonialism, to reject the maid but accept the [colonial] master would be illogical. In any case, because anthropology as a discipline can also be used to assist Africa in the contemporary struggles for decolonisation, to reject the discipline amounts to throwing the baby out with the bathwater. Rejecting anthropology on the premise that it was used by colonists to colonise Africans is paradoxical because the logic underlying this rejection would be expected to also apply to Africans who collaborated with colonists. In other words, logically those who collaborated with colonists would also have to be rejected and thrown out of the continental boat because they were so used, and arguably used much more intensively than anthropology as a discipline.

The point is therefore to adopt the discipline but keep eyes open on the ulterior motives of Western funders of the discipline(s) and researches within it and across disciplines. Funders often dictate the aims, objectives and theories to be used in researching yet this dictation militate not only against African academics' freedoms but it also militates against the latter and spirit of African liberation more broadly. The politics of disciplines and research are, thus, important to note since the discipline is not only entangled in national politics but in the academic politics of research that dumb down African freedoms to reroute the discipline of anthropology towards supporting contemporary decolonial liberation struggles on the continent.

Universities across the world have various research fellowships and funding and in fact some of the funding is extended by Western universities to African universities many of which (African universities), because of dire financial constraints, readily accept the funding even if the ulterior motives for the funds are not sufficiently scrutinised. While anthropology is affected by the politics attendant to researches and research fellowships and funding that is framed and directed by Western academies and corporations, the problem is obviously much broader and includes other disciplines as well. Thus, while in English it is said in proverbs: "look before you leap" African researchers including anthropologists often accept research funding without sufficient scrutiny of the ulterior motives of the funders. In this case it is a matter of relying on anthropologists who are not wizened including by African cultural anthropological axioms and proverbs.

Underlying assumptions of contemporary anthropological theoretical turns

Having looked at the historical trajectory of politics around the recognition of anthropology, it is now necessary to also look at the underlying assumptions of contemporary anthropological and indeed broader disciplinary theoretical turns. The first aspect that needs attention is the resurgence of global colonial discourses of animism that are aimed to popularise ideas about the vitality and subjectivity of objects.

While the purported intention is to liberate objects from human ownership and control, the nefarious effect of the gospel of animism is to deny Africans the ownership of their resources for which they engaged in anticolonial wars. While this purported liberation of objects from human ownership appears on the face of it to be acts of benevolence, the actual effects would be to defuse and pre-empt African struggles and struggles of peoples of the global south [in general] who are reclaiming their cultural artefacts and other materialities [lying in metropolitan centres] that have been looted during colonialism.

Africans as indeed other peoples in the global south have since the past few years intensified their struggles to get back their cultural artefacts; material tangible and intangible heritages. Though contemporary variants of anthropology that are funded by Western corporations, institutions and academies are presented in terms of revitalisation of indigenous knowledges, in terms of decoloniality of anthropology and so on, there is need to be cautious about the kinds of anthropology that are resurging. In short, the types of anthropology that popularise animism, vitalities, subject-subject as opposed to subject-object ontologies are intended by the funders to defeat or undermine contemporary African reclamations of their tangible and intangible heritages. The modus operandi is to first of all portray the tangible and intangible heritages as subjects [and not objects] and then purport to grant them autonomous rights that would undo African struggles for ownership and control of such tangible and intangible heritages.

Put in another way, contemporary anthropology as dictated from the West threatens to be as colonial as the colonial anthropology that has been rejected in many African academies. But the way to resist the abuse of anthropology is not to reject the discipline for the same would be advocated for when it comes to science, especially physics and chemistry which though beneficial to humanity have caused much damage in other spheres of life. One can think of the 1945 bombs at Nagasaki and Hiroshima which are all nefarious works of science. Instead, the way to resist the abuse of anthropology is to establish the discipline and then use it to correct the misrepresentations. If anthropology continues to be directed from imperial global centres as is currently with the case of African studies, it risks perpetuating irrelevance in African liberation and restitution struggles. In other words, while decoloniality is a relevant concept to contemporary African struggles, if contemporary Western anthropology disinherits Africans via ideologies of subject-subject ontologies designed to deny African ownership of their resources, then such contemporary anthropology in effect repeats the same old colonial practices of disinheriting Africans. The much celebrated subject-subject ontologies are not in fact meant to liberate Africans but to open up lacunae for the (neo-)colonial disinheriting of Africans via the purported subject-subject ontologies of relations. In this sense, it is not for the love of indigenous knowledges that Western academies and corporations are sponsoring indigenous knowledge researches and [African] studies; rather the intention is to sugar-coat the (neo-)colonial disinheritance of Africans with vacuous glorification of indigenous knowledge systems that are distorted to suit new imperialist purposes.

Furthermore, contemporary theoretical trajectories such as those that claim *flatness* of Africa, *openness* of the continent and absence of hierarchy on the continent (Latour, 2005) have the effect of rehashing and repeating the colonial ideologies that are traceable to John Locke (Parekh, 1995) who portrayed Africa and other colonial territories as empty space to be occupied by the colonists. Contemporary portrayals of Africa as *open* replicate Locke's notions of *empty space* which is open for (neo-)colonists to occupy. Contemporary theorisation of Africa as flat and as without hierarchies replicate Locke's ideas that Africa and other colonial territories did not have political hierarchical societies with Kings and chiefs. These ideologies that are rehashed and replicated are meant to justify and legitimise recolonisation which is being re-presented as decolonisation. Adequate scrutiny would reveal the fact that these contemporary ideologies masquerading as theories about openness for societies, flatness of societies, animism, subject-subject ontologies and so on are in fact imperial ideologies repackaged for the twenty-first century colonial ventures.

The contemporary recolonisation is already ongoing with Western transnational corporations grabbing land from impoverished African peasants. The land that is grabbed from African peasants is portrayed as open and therefore empty space in spite of it belonging to African peasants. Thus, the African peasants are not deemed to be human beings occupying the land but rather they are treated as animals and hence not deemed to deserve even compensation or consultation prior to the transnational corporation land grabs. Considered in terms of animism as indistinct from animals, the African peasants are being ignored and treated as without human rights in the ongoing transnational land grabs on the continent of Africa.

Thus, if John Locke's (Parekh, 1995) colonial ideologies presented the colonised world as without knowledge and distinction of who is an insider and who is an outsider, contemporary theories are presenting Africa and the global south as open societies. While Locke presented the colonised world as *terra nullius*, contemporary theories are presenting the colonised world as open. Although Locke presented the colonised world as *res nullius* or without notions of ownership, contemporary theories present the global south as possessing subject-subject ontologies that leave no room for ownership. Locke presented the colonised world as without political society including Kings and chiefs, but contemporary theories present the colonised world as flat and without hierarchy. All these aspects indicate that contemporary Western theories that are popularised in Western driven anthropology and other disciplines are in fact old colonial theories that are rehashed and hidden and re-presented as decolonial, modern, progressive theories.

If we look at the contemporary aversions and antipathy to African and other colonised peoples' genealogies and descent, these are traceable to colonial ideologies of animism where Africans were deemed to be animals without entitlements to their own families, their own marriage system, without entitlements to their own ancestry and genealogies and history (Nhemachena, 2016a). For instance, extreme [sexual] libertarianism has the effect of marginalising and undoing ancestry, marriage systems, family systems and genealogies. Anthropology, as indeed any discipline, no matter how much it is celebrated as postcolonial, that continues to deconstruct African families, marriages, genealogies and ancestry is in fact a replication of colonial anthropology. Sadly, much of postcolonial disciplines including anthropology have since the ascendancy of poststructuralism and postmodernism in the 1960s, focused on deconstructing African institutions thereby accentuating colonial anthropology (Nhemachena, 2016a).

In the contemporary politics around globalisation, anthropology of the margins has been stretched by discourses around the particular and the universal which on one hand condemned the particular and on the other hand glorified the universal. The binaries around the universal and the particular, by extension, condemned the African cultures, families, marriages, polities, societies as contra the universal, meaning the global north, especially the West and North America. The popularity of studying anthropology was obviously unhinged by discourses that condemned the objects of anthropological studies, that is, the particularities of Africa. Similarly, contemporary Western discourses that portray Africans as without essence, in effect diminish the essence of anthropology as a discipline equipped to study African essence. Closely following these condemnations of anthropology came the discourses that popularised hyper reality (Nhemachena, 2016a) and surrealism in the process denying the existence of real African cultures, societies, polities, identities, marriages, families and so on. Denial of the existence of reality had negative implications on anthropological objects of studies. If there is no real African cultures, African essences, heritages, societies, polities, marriages, families and so on, then what does anthropology got to study in Africa?

Conclusion

There is a lot of politics around the possibility of (re-)introducing the discipline of anthropology in African academies. While anthropology could have been used by colonists as their handmaiden, the political processes and exigencies of reconciliation also necessitate a parallel disciplinary epistemic reconciliation. There are many other disciplines that were used by colonists and therefore it does not make sense to single out anthropology and exclude it from the academic community of disciplines. It is therefore necessary to introduce anthropology in African academies and adapt it to the contemporary bona fide postcolonial and decolonial projects that can assist Africans to free themselves from contemporary global matrices of power.

Chapter 4

Anthropology and the Search for Relevance

Introduction

During the colonial era, as indeed in the contemporary era marked by globalisations forces, Africa had to be forced to be relevant [and hence beneficial] to colonial empire. Africans were given colonial names and their own African names were either struck off or subordinated to the Western names that became prevalent. Whereas African names were meaningful and relevant to the African contexts, since they were meaningful and of relevance in ancestral ritual invocations and they served as mnemonic devices, Western names that were enforced served to make Africa relevant to the imperial colonial exploitative relationships. In addition to being given these colonial names, Africans were also studied using western theories, categories and terms that were not relevant to the wellbeing of local indigenous people.

Apart from this, African traditional medicines were exploited by the imperial colonial establishment. Africans were thus made to believe that African traditional medicine was of irrelevance to their wellbeing as colonists sought to supplant Africans from their own institutions. African medicine was vilified and condemned by colonists and the missionaries that operated as colonial emissaries. Yet the colonial imperial system paradoxically exploited African traditional medicines in the production of their own medicines which they then dispensed in hospitals and clinics. With the imposition of colonial systems, African political, economic and religious systems were squeezed out of African contexts. African chiefs were superseded by colonial native commissioners who determined and imposed irrelevant colonial policies on African anthropic desiderata ensuring in the process that African chiefs that agreed or acquiesced to serve the colonial establishments became irrelevant to African aspirations for sovereignty, autonomy and liberation. In all these colonial imperial machinations, anthropology was complicity as often there were collaborations between anthropologists and colonial administrators, and anthropological researches fed into the colonial imperial system providing crucial information for the colonial imperial administrators (Nhemachena *et al* 2016a). For these reasons, the relevance of the discipline of anthropology to postcolonial Africa became an issue resulting in many African scholars and political leaders arguing for the discipline to be wiped out of the African academies.

Anthropology and colonial relevance

Much as some scholars have linked anthropology to the Nazi holocaust, others have also linked anthropology to the colonisation of the African continent and the genocides that were perpetrated on African people, such as the Herero and the Nama in Namibia, in the early years of colonialism. Anthropologists spent time in the field studying Africans generating immense information that was significant for the efficient administration of the colonies. This role of anthropology is well captured by Ntarangwi *et al* (2006: 9) who argue that: "At the most general level, most anthropologists were members of European societies that participated enthusiastically in the imperial project and so share some responsibility for the patronising moral attitudes and exploitative social relations it espoused. At a more individual level, there were many who sought to develop a critique of these relations…"

For Ntarangwi *et al* (2006: 8): "The ideological shadow of western influence…continues to delegitimise anthropology". In this sense, anthropologists are often linked to espionage and spying on African institutions for purposes of providing information to the colonial imperial establishment. Thus, anthropologists such as Isaac Schapera, Philip Gulliver, Grillo were tasked with looking into ways in which colonial governments could benefit from anthropology, to see how anthropology could provide avenues for colonial indirect rule and to work as consultants for the colonial governments. This can be understood in terms of the fact that the colonial institutions and organisations that funded anthropological researches needed to make profits from the colonies and hence to effectively control and govern the African populations resident in those colonies.

In Zimbabwe, the British South Africa Company (BSACo) together with the architect of the colonisation of the territory, Cecil John Rhodes, sponsored researches that were meant to be relevant for the colonisers' subjugation and administration of the colony. Researches were sponsored to generate propaganda about the monuments, researches were also sponsored to generate propaganda about backwardness and absence of development and of industries in Africa as ways to justify and legitimise colonial establishments. Even as they knew about Timbuktu and other African centres of learning and teaching, colonial imperial researchers dismissed Africa as lacking education and academies; these researchers were justifying their relevance not to Africa but to the colonial imperial establishments that funded their researches and the academies that educated them. Anthropologists as practitioners and thinkers at the frontiers between the colonial establishments and the African people sometimes prevaricated and infringed the colonial scholarly injunctions not to turn native and begin to sympathise with the natives.

The irrelevance [to Africans] of colonial anthropology was partly explained by the colonial injunctions that anthropologists who studied natives had to desist from turning native; it was an anthropology in which anthropologists had to desist from becoming sympathetic and emotional towards the African colonial subjects being subjected to multiple form of colonial dispossession. The assumption of dispassionate objective, contextless research partly explains the irrelevance of the discipline to African colonial subjects that were made to believe that colonial researchers were dispassionate and objective. African colonial subjects would have expected anthropologists to be more sympathetic and to assist them to effectively resist colonisation but they were in fact enjoined by the colonial scholarly rubrics to be "dispassionate" and "objective", and "emotionless" and which in fact meant that they had to be irrelevant to Africans. The injunction to be "dispassionate" and "objective" in studying African colonial subjects was in fact an injunction not to be sympathetic to the victims of colonisation or imperialism who were being exploited as cheap/unpaid labour, disinherited by the colonial systems that expropriated their livestock, land children and women; they were being disinherited by the fact that the colonial system destroyed their cultures, religions, polities, economies and societies. It was by extension an injunction to anthropologists to be irrelevant to the people that they researched.

In spite of these critiques, Ntarangwi *et al* (2006: 19) write noting the utility of anthropology to Africans: "Whilst one may wish to dismiss anthropology as an intimate part of a colonial knowledge structure, one also has to acknowledge the interstitial space that the discipline offered to those of a critical bent, both nurturing an anti-colonial consciousness and inviting the first steps in Africanising the discipline. It was, indeed, anthropology's role as the 'sociology of primitive people' that allowed social scientists to engage with people that were often overlooked or neglected by other social sciences (sociologists, economists and political scientists, just to name a few), and in turned equipped, these African leaders with the social and cultural data necessary to demand informed politico-economic changes for the citizenry".

The questions of relevance of [colonial] anthropology can be analysed in terms of branches of anthropology such as political, cultural, medical, economic, environmental, physical/biological anthropology. The questions of relevance can also be analysed in terms of the scientism of enlightenment thought that characterised the beginning of the discipline. The philosophies of Spinoza and others that categorised the world in terms of hierarchies of humanity in which Africans were deemed to be closest to animals and other brutes of nature; the scientism that dismissed African religion as devil worship or as figments of imagination outside scientific cannons all made anthropologists patronisingly derisory of African institutions. The effect was that the anthropology was less to understand Africans than it was to model and frame them in terms of Western epistemologies and in terms of ongoing colonial projects.

Firstly, physical and biological anthropology greatly assisted in understanding African societies but there were challenges to the deployment of such a branch of anthropology on Africa. In so far as it explained the origin of human beings in terms of the Darwinist evolution processes, physical/biological anthropology side-tracked African explanations of human origin in terms of creation *ex nihilo* by God, known by different names across the continent since precolonial era (Ntholi 2006). Explanations of life in terms of the scientific big bang are still popular in academies on the continent that continue to look down on African explanations of life and the world in terms of creation by God. In fact, explanations of the origins of human beings in terms of creation by God have come to be derisively addressed by evolutionists as *creationism*.

Explanations of human origins in terms of the Darwinist evolution not only helped some anthropologists remove God from the matrix of African societies but they also helped place Africans at the lowest rung of human evolution as understood by colonial scholars. Placing Africans at the lowest rungs of evolution served to legitimise researching them as curios of the past, as half humans still struggling to exit the animal kingdom. It served the colonial/imperial establishment that then found legitimacy not only in capturing, enslaving and colonising Africans but also in shipping them off to Europe to serve as entertainment in human zoos where they were kept together with animals such as monkeys, baboons and so on (Nhemachena 2016b). Some contemporary scholars are revitalising [irrelevant] discourses of animism that, underlie Darwinism in their presupposition that Africans are not only related to animals but not distinct from animals.

Evolutionary anthropology also served to legitimise dispossession of Africans who, having been depicted as half human and very close to animals, were deemed not to be capable of owning anything (Nhemachena 2016b). Thus, the logics of fields of "development" studies, "modernisation" and so on are premised on evolutionism and on assumptions that Africans are still backward and close to nature [including animals] and therefore they need to be "assisted" to get out of the backwardness and animality via "development", "modernisation" and "civilisation". Evolutionary anthropology therefore assisted in legitimising colonists' missions of "civilisation", "development" and "modernisation". Evolutionary anthropology assisted in legitimising race science that erroneously considered Africans to be 'intellectually inferior' and thus to have 'lower intelligent quotients' as compared to whites and other races.

Secondly, political anthropology helped to legitimise colonial conquest by for instance presupposing that Africans had no political systems and that they were always in perpetual, interminable striving for life. Colonial anthropology based on Hobbesian theories that presupposed the absence of governments prior to colonisation manufactured figments of 'tribal' chaos and crises on the continent and they served to legitimise and glorify colonisers as 'peacemakers' on otherwise fractious 'tribes' and ethnic groups. This kind of anthropology [with foundations in Hobbesian theories] unfortunately continues to be peddled thereby legitimising the meddlesomeness of former colonisers on the pretext of helping pacify African anarchic and chaotic "tribes".

On the basis of colonially manufactured notions of 'tribalism' and 'ethnicity', Africans were not only portrayed as traditional and backward but they were portrayed as locked up in perpetual warfare and raids in the colonially assumed absence of laws, norms and social cohesion. Ranger's (1989) work on how colonists invented traditions and 'ethnicity' for purposes of dividing and ruling, taming and controlling Africans, is informative. The colonially invented notions of 'tribalism' are resilient in Africa and have been so internalised by some African scholars that they cannot help but replicate in their writings the categorisation and interpellation, 'tribe'. Some Africans interpellated and hailed by the colonially manufactured terms, 'tribe', have resorted to wars on the basis of the colonial categories even in postcolonial context. The wars in Rwanda, Kenya, Sudan and Somalia still constantly conjure up premises of 'tribalism' and 'ethnicity' long after the colonists that created these categories have left.

Of course in the media, including western media reports, academics and journalists still use the terms like 'tribes' in reference to Africans. These divisive terms like 'tribalism' and 'ethnicity' ignore the unity and cohesion in pre-colonial Africa that existed on the basis of communal rituals as well as on the basis of extraterritorial pilgrimages such as to the *Mwari* (God) shrines at the Matopo Hills in Zimbabwe (MacGonagle 2007; Ntholi 2006; Werbner 1989). Different groups of African people such as the Venda, Ndau, Ndebele, Shona, Kalanga and even some groups of people from Zambia, Botswana, Mozambique and South Africa regularly made pilgrimages to the Matopo Hills to pray to *Mwari* (God) and these pilgrimages united them [not in terms of colonial tribes but] as African people generally. The point therefore is that colonial anthropology was relevant to the colonial establishment in so far as it depicted Africans as 'tribes' and other colonial divisive categories; in this respect the anthropology was not relevant to the cause of Africans who strove for unity across the colonially fabricated categories. Therefore the Shona and Ndebele uprisings, in spite of huge swathes of land in Zimbabwe, saw both the Shona and Ndebele people uniting to fight the invading colonists. The categories of 'tribe' and 'ethnicity' had no relevance in the collective resistance by the Shona and Ndebele people against colonisers; the categories like 'tribe' were not material in the uprisings by the indigenous Africans, and therefore they were irrelevant colonial categories.

Thirdly, economic anthropology played its role in support of the colonial establishment in so far as it presupposed that Africans were economically backward, lacking industries, innovations and development. These portrayals served to legitimise destruction of African industries. Africans had industries such as mining, smelting, music/entertainment, beer brewing, carpentry, basketry, health services, education, weaving, agriculture including crop cultivation and animal husbandry, African could build and therefore has great architectural skills that colonists were keen to suppress and appropriate (Ellert 1984; Schmidt 1992; Posselt 1935). The Africans also had trade/commerce within the continent and beyond, yet the colonists were keen to destroy these as a step to capturing Africans and exploiting them as unpaid labour in their own [colonists] industries. Anthropology in so far as it largely portrayed Africans as without industries and as backward was relevant to the colonial system. Up to today, many anthropologists continue to assume that the category *subsistence* belongs naturally to Africans; thus they ignore the impressive array of evidence from archaeology, anthropology and history that show that Africans had commercial industries well before colonist invaded the continent. In much economic anthropology there are uncritical assumptions that industry properly and naturally belongs to colonists, westerners and their progeny and that Africans have never had knowledge about how to run and create industries, including commerce.

This kind of anthropology is of little, if any, relevance to Africa as it ignores the realities of the continent.

Fourthly, cultural anthropology has tended to depict Africans as cultural others in Said's (1973) sense of Occidentalism and orientalism. African culture has been depicted by anthropologists as cultures without 'civilisation' or as 'backward', 'savage', 'barbaric' cultures destined for extinction with the march of western 'civilisation'. In this sense, cultural anthropology also served to legitimise the colonial mission *civilisatrice*. Thus, in spite of the fact that African architecture including grass thatched huts were appropriate for the hot climates since grass is a bad conductor of heat [thus ensuring that the huts remain cool during the hot summers, and remains warm during cold winters] African architecture was demonised as 'uncivilised' and 'backward'. Some have proceeded to construct corrugated iron roofed houses believing that was not only better but progressively modern but they have sadly realised that such sheets are very hot in summers and very cold in winters, since metals are conductors of heat. They have had therefore to spend more than they anticipated on installing roof ceilings.

In spite of the fact that African cultural circumcision rites were beneficial, they were summarily demonised as 'backward', 'savage' and 'barbaric' in colonial anthropological treatises. The fact that in the contemporary era, even the World Health Organisation is promoting circumcision underscores the irrelevance of colonial cultural anthropology especially that which condemned African circumcision rituals as 'barbaric' and 'savage'. Similarly, the condemnation of African marriages, families and education systems has seen complex problems arising in African societies as many struggles [to the extent of even seeking the services of healers and prophets] in vain to secure marriages, to ensure marriages and families last. The problems such as of street children and youths have arisen in a context where African marriage and family systems have been summarily condemned by those colonial anthropologists and others that studied these institutions. Similarly, problems of rape, marital and family violence have risen and multiplied in context where some scholars that studied these African institutions summarily condemned the African institutions that controlled rape, governed marriages and families. What all this entails is that relevance requires patience as much as it requires proper lenses to see cultures on the basis of their own premises.

Fifthly, medical anthropology has traditionally dismissed African indigenous health systems. As in the case of other branches of anthropology, such medical anthropology served and was of relevance to the colonial system that was keen to prevent competition between African health systems and colonists' health services provisions. Colonial anthropology had to be relevant in supporting the colonial health systems that were keen to generate business out of African clients; but after turning Africans away from their own competing health systems. Implied in this is the fact that colonial medical anthropology was of little relevance to Africans whose own medical systems the colonists summarily demonised and discouraged. This irrelevance of foisted colonial medical anthropology has resulted in Africans losing knowledge about their own indigenous medical systems and preferring to use the colonial western medical systems. These colonial western medical systems are however expensive and inaccessible to the greater majority of Africans who have been impoverished by the same colonial systems. In a contemporary context where inclusion has become the buzz word, anthropology that excludes and uncritically demonises African indigenous medical systems has no relevance for Africans struggling day and night to access medical services including where western medical systems have collapsed. Still on the area of medical anthropology and its relevance in the betterment of Africans, colonial medical systems that discouraged Africans from eating traditional [organic] herbs have been of little relevance to the health of Africans. The fact that herbs and organic foods, often also traditional, are now being encouraged by dieticians indicates that the anthropology that discouraged Africans from consuming such organic foods and herbs is irrelevant for the lives of Africans many of whom were encouraged to prefer western refined, chemically preserved food stuff.

Sixthly, in the realm of environmental anthropology, the relevance of anthropology that condemned African spirituality as 'backward' and 'uncivilised' is being questioned. The fact that African spirituality is central to contemporary African ecotheology and conservation measures speaks volumes about the irrelevance of anthropological works that historically condemned such spirituality. Ecotheology has become a huge resource for conservation of African environments where western and colonial systems of conservation have failed to preserve and conserve African environments. African spirituality, in so far as it supports totemism, has also played a huge role in conservation of environments, including biodiversity. Thus colonial anthropology, in so far as it demonised African spirituality and totemism, was on little relevance for environmental conservation practices in Africa.

As argued by scholars like Francis Nyamnjoh (2012a) the problem with colonial anthropology is that it was manned by anthropologists who were in fact evangelists of western epistemologies. Instead of engaging in [mutual] *conversation* with

Africans, the colonial evangelist scholars privileged *converting* Africans to the colonial project. For this reason colonial anthropology was not relevant in *conversing* with and understanding Africans, rather it was relevant in *converting* Africans so that they would become colonial docile and domesticated subjects.

One example that shows the irrelevance of colonial anthropology in engaging in conversation with and understanding Africans is the colonial mistranslation of ceremonies conducted by Africans to request for rain. Many [colonial] anthropologists have mistranslated, misunderstood and misrepresented these ceremonies calling them "rainmaking ceremonies" when in fact careful attention to and conversation with Africans would have revealed that the Africans do not claim to engage in 'rainmaking' ceremonies but rather in their ceremonies, they petition or request for rain. They request for rain via their *mhondoro*, or great grand forebears who are considered to be close to God and thus to relay the concerns or requests to God for rain to come. Although many anthropologists studying these ceremonies have erroneously called them 'rainmaking' ceremonies, for the Shona people of Zimbabwe the ceremonies are called *mukwerera* and they involve petitioning for rain rather than 'making the rain'; they do not attempt to 'make rain' but they request for it (Nhemachena, 2013; 2014). What these shortfalls of colonial anthropology mean is that often when anthropologists privilege *conversion* over *conversation* with Africans, we tend to hear more the voices and opinions of the anthropologists rather than the voices of the Africans being studied. The anthropologists that privilege *conversion* over *conversation* therefore produce irrelevant anthropology for the Africans that they claim to study.

These shortcomings of colonial anthropology are clearly shown by Diana Jeater's (2007) book wherein she portrays the challenges that colonial anthropologists had in engaging, understanding and representing African societies. *N'anga* or traditional healers have been mistranslated by colonial anthropologists as 'witchdoctors' even though their work is not principally in dealing with witches as indeed they do a great deal of work (re)connecting Africans with their ancestors; giving medicines to treat ailments; they act as counsellors in families and communities where there are conflicts and they advise on what rituals to perform in matters of marriages, illnesses, childbirth, death etc. In spite of all these functions, colonial anthropologists portrayed the *n'anga* as 'witchdoctors'. Other colonial anthropologists portrayed them as 'bone-throwers' even if the *n'anga* do not necessarily engage in 'bone-throwing', but rather some use sticks for purposes of divination. Jeater (2007) further shows translation challenges that colonial anthropologists had in the areas of [customary] indigenous law which has since the colonial era been ossified and rigidified in spite of the fact that it was fluid and not rigid in pre-colonial African societies.

These challenges, by colonial anthropologists, in engaging and understanding African societies attenuate the relevance of colonial anthropology in Africa. The challenges entail the need to revisit colonial anthropology and that colonial anthropological works need not constitute 'bibles' for contemporary postcolonial African anthropologists. African anthropologists need to reengage colonial anthropological works and interrogate them for relevance, truth and facticity; there is need not to take their facticity for granted particularly given the partnership colonial anthropology had with colonial imperial establishments and projects to convert Africans into empire's projects.

The need for intellectual vigilance by African anthropologists is necessitated by the observation that: "African anthropology continues to be characterised by an imbalance in its disciplinary networks: The international networks that are a legacy of colonial rule outweigh the regional and national networks...It is instructive that anthropologists in Africa communicate less across national boundaries within Africa than they do with colleagues in Europe and North America or Australia" (Ntarangwi *et al* 2006: 29).

In spite of the above challenge, Ntarangwi *et al* (2006: 33) further cite Marcus and Fischer's (1986) argument that: " In its practice, African anthropology can decentre western epistemological traditions by unpacking African ways of knowing, creating its own traditions of reflexive anthropology and cultural critique".

What this means is that relevance is a question of whether one privileges and foregrounds the African epistemologies and ontologies or on the other hand whether one foreground and privileges the western epistemologies and ontologies. Sadly much anthropological works continue to privilege and foreground western theories, concepts and categories when researching and seeking to understand Africa. Such scholars, Francis Nyamnjoh (2012a) describes as *excelling in irrelevance.*

Chapter 5

Anthropology in Zimbabwe Thirty-Five Years after Independence

Introduction

The situation for anthropology in Zimbabwe is well captured by Ntarangwi *et al.'s* (2006: 28) observation that: Anthropologists are usually 'hidden' within sociology departments, and yet most of the empirical research done for the masters and doctorates in countries such as Namibia, Botswana and Zimbabwe is carried out by anthropologists". Joint departments of sociology and anthropology are found in many African countries and so: "Within Anglophone Africa there are very few academic institutions with autonomous anthropology departments" (Ntarangwi *et al* 2006: 23).

Although anthropological works by scholars like Charles Bullock; Michael Gelfand; Elizabeth Colson; Michael Bourdillon; Richard Werbner; Elizabeth MacGonagle; Gordon Chavunduka; Victor Muzvidziwa; Solomon Mombeshora and others exist, a younger generation of anthropologists needs to be mentored to carry the discipline forward. Books and articles on marriages, family life, culture, medical anthropology, political anthropology, religions of the inhabitants of Zimbabwe, environment, social change and effects of colonisation on the peoples of Zimbabwe, rituals and so on have already been published since the colonial era. However as noted by Muzvidziwa (2006) and Zeleza (1997: iv) cited in Ntarangwi (2006), the strong ethnographic tradition has been limited by a weaker theoretical base, a drawback that has characterised the teaching of anthropology up to the present day.

The challenge with an ethnographic slant lacking any theoretical base is that analytical rigour is compromised by absence of theory. Without theory, the ethnographic studies become mere narratives, explorations or descriptive ventures that do not carry the anthropological analysis any further. If we are to borrow Tim Ingold's (2008) argument that anthropology is not ethnography, mere descriptive ethnographies without theorisation are not necessarily anthropological ventures. Anthropology is also about theorising using the ethnographic data and so ethnography does not automatically translate to anthropology. What this entails is that for one to claim to be an anthropologist, one has to know and apply anthropological theory to ethnography.

Bewailing lack of theorisation, and hence lack of anthropology in spite of African ethnography, Zeleza (1997: iv) [cited in Ntarangwi (2006: 31] argues thus: "Their countries and communities cry out for clear and committed analyses, not the superficial travelogues they often get from foreign fly-by-night academic tourists". If we read this argument together with the fact that many African academics including anthropologists are surviving on the basis of consultancies (Mamdani 2011; Ntarangwi *et al* 2006) where scholarly creativity is sacrificed to survival necessities, it become more evident that African scholars have been engaging more in ethnography than anthropology in the decades after independence.

Although with the postcolonial era [since the 1970s], the colonised have been granted voice, the fact that anthropology has been condemned as the handmaiden of colonialism explains the scholarly throes in which the discipline found itself. While the condemnation of anthropology as a handmaiden of colonialism has some justification, the lack of popularity of anthropology in post-independence Africa meant that post-independence Africa lost an opportunity provided by the spaces that were opened for multivocality, plurivocality and heteroglossia that would have allowed as many Africans to research, write anthropology making their voices heard. The scratching off and or marginalisation of anthropology in post-independence Africa did little to provide for spaces to correct the misrepresentations of Africa by colonial anthropologists.

Since anthropology is by its nature interdisciplinary, the uncorrected misrepresentations of colonial anthropology continued to filter into other disciplines with which anthropology has connections. Thus students of history, environment studies, political science, sociology, ecology, theology, geography, media and information, law and development studies continue to refer to Africans in terms of colonial categories such as 'tribes', 'underdeveloped' and hence 'backward', 'uncivilised', 'savage'. Many students of theology, history, environmental studies, development studies, geography continue to view and portray [following scholars like James Frazer (1926)] Africans as 'animists'. They continue to view and portray Africans as unable to distinguish between themselves as human beings and animals/nature; they continue to view and portray Africans as without the notion of a transcendental God and they continue to view and portray Africans as worshippers of ancestors, rather than worshippers of God. As noted in the previous chapter these colonial views and portrayals of animism were relied upon to justify the colonisation of Africans that were depicted first by colonists as indistinct from animals and hence incapable of owning property (Nhemachena 2016b).

Because the discipline of anthropology receded or stagnated in post-independence Africa, not much of colonial anthropological misrepresentations have been corrected and so the colonial misrepresentations continue to infect postcolonial African minds. Colonial anthropological caricaturing of African cultures continues but from the forts of other cognate disciplines that haven't benefited from anthropological self-corrections and reflexivity. Thus African marriages continue to be demonised in mainstream scholarly productions in spite of evidence that in everyday life many Africans are hankering for respite in the African-revered institutions like marriage and family. Evidence is abounding that many ordinary Africans go even to the extents of consulting traditional healers and prophets for remedies when they fail to get married and to establish families. Some evidence exists that some who exit marriages and families by divorce get so pained that they commit suicide. Yet the institutions are demonised by mainstream scholars feeding on age-old colonial anthropological portrayals and demonization of African institutions. Many on the continent still rely heavily on marriages and families for their social security particularly because the western institutions of social security, as much as they have never been meant to provide for everyone, have also receded and crumbled (Nhemachena 2016c).

Western education has not delivered its promises to endow those who pass with jobs and so post-independence Africa needs anthropologists to work as *bricoleurs* in Levi-Strauss' (1970) sense and put the pieces that were broken by colonial establishments together for Africa to resurface 'alternatives' social security, health provision, family set up and marriage set ups. Because anthropology receded after independence, a lot still needs to be done to track environmental including climate change to provide 'alternative' stories to western ones on climate and environmental change. African rituals are still viewed largely as 'uncivilised' and 'backward' in spite of mammoth failure of the colonists, who in fact worsened the African conditions by exploiting, expropriation and externalisation of resources while shooting down African intangible heritages in the form of rituals.

In post-independence Zimbabwe, anthropologists like Gordon Lloyd Chavunduka assisted the Zimbabwe National Traditional Healers Association get recognition through an Act of Parliament that was initially heavily resisted by some parliamentarians who thought that legislating in favour of the constitution of the healers' organisation was retrogressive and savage (Waite 2000). However the healers proved helpful and to be a resource for the majority of the population, particularly after the introduction of Economic Structural Adjustment Programme that saw formal health sector crumbling with incessant strikes by health personnel and incessant shortages of drugs. In the most recent crises in Zimbabwe which also acutely affected the health sector, traditional healers and traditional medicine proved to offer valuable fall-back positions for millions of Zimbabweans affected by the collapse of the formal health sector.

In spite of the utility of traditional medicine and healers, the institution continues after independence to face demonization particularly by some Pentecostal churches who, even in their preaching, continue to address traditional healers and African ancestors as demons. They address herbal medicines provided by healers as demonic even if the pills and other drugs in the hospitals and clinic are also made from herbs, roots and leaves of trees and shrubs. Some demonise healers and Africans in general as having had no knowledge to quantify medicines, despite precolonial existence of African indigenous mathematics. The implication is that there is still a lot that postcolonial Zimbabwean and African anthropologists can do to educate critics of Africa who rely on colonial anthropological misrepresentations of Africans as illiterate and lacking numerical skills. Scholars in other parts of the world are pursuing discoveries of indigenous mathematics or what others call 'ethnomathematics' that have been relied upon by Africans for centuries prior to colonisation. Such mathematical knowledge is evident in Zimbabwean for instance Shona culture where there are indigenous vernacular names for numbers [such as *imwechete* for one; *mbiri* for two; *nhatu* for three; *ina* for four; *shanu* for five; *nhanhatu* for six; *nomwe* for seven; *sere* for eight and *pfumbamwe* for nine and *gumi* for ten etc.). Furthermore, the Zimbabwe monuments exhibit great knowledge not only of architecture but also of mathematics, including geometry that need to be studied and theorised including by anthropologists.

As Muzvidziwa (2006) observes, the problem in postcolonial anthropology is that its teaching has undergone significant changes and shifts without breaking from its past. Postcolonial anthropology continues largely to follow colonial trajectories in a context where colonial education has remained resilient in Francis Nyamnjoh's (2012a) sense.

The precolonial African abilities to weave (Schmidt 1992; Ellert 1984) presuppose mathematical knowledge; African abilities for basketry, crocheting, moulding clay pots and plates presume knowledge of mathematics including geometrical principles. In spite of the fact that Africans in precolonial Zimbabwe could manufacture guns (Ellert 1984), postcolonial anthropologists have not researched this so as to produced textbooks about African knowledge and practices, in the areas of technology. In spite of these abilities, anthropologists have not done enough in post-independence Zimbabwe and Africa to surface these knowledges and abilities by Africans. Africans continue to read and rely on colonial texts that were calculated to induce feeling of inferiority and inadequacy in the peoples of the continent. The recession of anthropology as a discipline in post-independence Africa and Zimbabwe was therefore unfortunate since anthropology is potentially powerful in restoring the dignity and colonial disinheritance that still yearns for interrogation and correction.

The unfortunate thing is that Africa continues decades after independence to be theorised from the west often via irrelevant concepts (Nyamnjoh 2012a): there is very little if any theorisation on the basis of African indigenous knowledge. From African politics to the most intimate realm of African sexualities, the Africans are theorised from western premises and concepts and so even though there are some African anthropologists that are still active on the continent, their works are unfortunately hamstrung by western theoretical caps. Thus, the challenge in postcolonial Zimbabwe and Africa is that the few anthropologists that remain are also trapped in the consultancy syndrome whereas Mamdani (2011) observes, they mostly serve as hunter-gatherers of raw data for NGOs and for Western scholars who provide funding for the researches on the continent. As hunter-gatherers of raw data they lack room not only to determine the research agendas and objectives but they also lack room to critically reflect on and theorise on the data which they produce. Thus the anthropologists continue to serve interests other than producing and correcting knowledge for Africa's sake. Because not much has been done in post-independence Africa and Zimbabwe to correct colonial anthropological misrepresentations, whichever NGOs and CSOs employ anthropologists design their research questions, objectives on the premises of uncorrected colonial misrepresentations of Africa and so the sad replication of misrepresentations continues.

The colonial misrepresentations of African life as 'backward', 'savage', 'miserable' and 'uncivilised' is in urgent need of attention by post-independence anthropologists. In post-independence Zimbabwe and Africa for instance, afflicted Africans continue to stress themselves with pressures to escape living in grass thatched huts even to the extent that they see life in shack as better than living in grass thatched huts in the middle of villages. In post-independence Africa, afflicted Africans continue to hanker for pilgrimages to the gravesites of the heroes of colonial history and paradoxically they seldom, if at all, ask questions about the gravesites of their own ancestors and grand forebears like Nehanda, Kaguvi, Karigamombe and others. The grave of the architect of colonisation of Zimbabwe, Cecil John Rhodes, continues to attract, both as a tourist attraction and a source of inspiration, people from all walks of life from near and far.

Because research agendas for postcolonial anthropologists continue to be set in the West, they have done little to research on and retrace African artefacts such as the Zimbabwe birds as well as the heads of African anticolonial resisters that were shipped off to Europe during the colonial era. In other words, because of the predominance of NGO consultancy research with agendas set elsewhere, very few African anthropologists are researching and writing for the sake of surfacing and developing national and continental heritage. In fact many have been turned by western theorists, who are against the African nation states, to write against their national heritages and peoples. African youths have been taught to self-despise and self-hate, and as evident in the Afrophobic violence in countries like South Africa, to hate fellow Africans even as they paradoxically prefer and welcome westerners. The westerners are thus declaring the national heritages to be world heritages often in much the same way colonists have *defacto* declared African artefacts to belong not to Africa but to the 'world'.

The question is about how post-independence anthropology can be made relevant first of all to Africans before we can talk about the 'world'. Much like colonial anthropology sought to be relevant to colonial imperial establishments before it could be to Africans, privileging the 'world' in place of relevance to Africans is in fact a repetition of the colonial nature of anthropology. The problem in disciplines such as anthropology is that Africans have come last and western funders of researches and academies have tended to come first. Hence African heritages are declared 'world' heritages even if such declarations make the heritages inaccessible to Africans.

The upshot here is that, Zimbabweans as indeed African anthropologists, are still to sufficiently locate themselves in the local where fieldwork occurs and then relating their results, experiences and imaginations to the broader global picture (Ntarangwi *et al* 2006: 3). The point here is that African anthropologists, in postcolonial Zimbabwe, need not savour merely on local delicacies of ethnographic minutiae that they then present to the 'world' as narratives devoid of imaginations beyond localities of origins.

Due to the colonial epistemologies and practices that inculcated in Africans senses of inadequacy and self-hatred, Africans have not only lost their material heritage but they have also lost their nonmaterial heritage since the colonial era.

Africans have lost their knowledge about performing rituals for marriages, birth, death, agriculture, rain, health, harvest and security. In other words, social security has come to be premised on what some scholars have understood as modern institutions that are very exclusionary particularly for the impoverished Africans. Besides, in post-independence contexts where the African states have lost policy space partly due to International Monetary Fund and World Bank imposed neoliberal programmes, social security provision in Africa have become extremely thin if not virtually non-existent for many.

In such contexts, Africa's majority of the population that is rural based continue to see relevance in rituals for instance in petitioning for rains particularly since the onset of the current climate change trajectory. Given the failure of Euro-modernist interventions including the failure of the international protocols on climate change and greenhouse emissions, endogenous knowledges and practices that are best captured by Anthropology provide alternatives. Similarly, Anthropology offers resources to understand and promote post-independence endogenous health practices that have ensured the survival of many particularly in crisis periods when modernist health provisions floundered. All these practices indicate the paradox that in post-independence Africa, Zimbabwe included, Anthropology has lost disciplinary traction exactly in an era when indigenous knowledges and practices assumed salience for many Africans afflicted by the vicissitudes of post-coloniality.

Many decades after independence in Zimbabwe, the discipline of Anthropology continue to be so marginalised that only two universities teach the discipline and they teach it subsumed under Sociology Department. Given the lack of funding for research in post-independence academies, funding for [long drawn] anthropological research in villages is non-existent. Even postgraduate students of Sociology who decide to research on some anthropological issues focus predominantly on researching conveniently contiguous urban societies, or urban anthropology to the virtual neglect of rural societies where the majority of African people live and where transformation is arguably needed the most. What is more, in a post-independence context where African epistemologies, religions, cultures and institutions, continue to be demonised as backward, students generally question the relevance of studying Anthropology for their material wellbeing, in terms of availability of jobs for anthropologists who with the demise of colonialism no longer have native commissioners to advise.

A good example of the state of the discipline in post-independence Zimbabwe can be drawn from one of the authors of this book, Dr Nhemachena's experiences soon after completing MSc studies is sociology and social anthropology. He suggested to some colleagues at one of the universities in Zimbabwe that as anthropologists we could establish a semi-autonomous research institute to study indigenous knowledge and while this received support from some, others considered the idea of indigenous knowledge to be backward. They considered the idea of indigenous knowledge so backward that in their eyes it would not bring material dividends to them. In spite of the contributions of indigenous knowledge to modern medicine and health for example, one colleague quibbled the question: "So who is going to be the chief native commissioner in the indigenous knowledge research institute?" Presupposed by the question is sadly that indigenous people always need and cannot do without native commissioners; and that researches of indigenous people have to be commissioned by native commissioners that have to be created if they happen to have expired with colonialism.

Given these challenges, Anthropology in postcolonial Zimbabwe, as indeed the rest of Africa, is studied by anthropologists based outside the countries and the continent and funded externally. It is good that anthropologists from outside continue to research and write African anthropology but the question is about the relevance of such externally funded and initiated anthropology to organic decolonial efforts or to postcolonial realities. In other words, the question for such externally sponsored anthropology as Nyamnjoh (2004) argues is whether those external funders that pay the anthropologist-pipers would ever stop calling the tune for those that they have paid. Thus, the issue is whether externally sponsored anthropology could conceivably be decolonial, postcolonial and relevant to those being researched and studied.

External funders of anthropological research have sadly often designed not only the research agendas for African anthropologists but they have also set the research templates for African anthropologists. Ntarangwi *et al* (2006: 35-6) therefore note: "There is an increasing reliance by funders and donors on a standardisation of research procedures with simplistic breakdown of the research and writing process into methodology, data collection, results and conclusions...Such chunky categories do not necessarily do justice to the nuances of anthropological knowledge, or the iterative process of carrying out anthropological research..."

As scholars like Oyewumi (2013) and Amadiume (1987; 2000) show about postcolonial Africa; anthropologists continue generally to foreground western categories that often cloud African realities. In this sense, anthropologists in postcolonial eras have largely continued to generate ignorance by uncritically imposing western categories on local realities that could otherwise be understood on their own local terms and categories (Nyamnjoh 2012a). Many African scholars have therefore criticised not only anthropology but social sciences in general as furthering imperialism. African universities have been understood as serving imperialism particularly where they foreground western epistemologies and practices rather than endogenous knowledges and practices.

Far from merely dismissing anthropology as colonial and imperial, the above critiques presuppose the need to deploy anthropology for remedial exercises in Africa. They presuppose the need to employ anthropology more extensively in doing corrections; in hunting for local endogenous terms and categories that can destabilise colonial terms and categories. In other words, postcolonial Zimbabwe and Africa more generally can be better off with an anthropology performing remedial exercises than without it.

Chapter 6

Debunking the Myths, Resuscitating the Discipline: The Future of Social Anthropology in Zimbabwe

Introduction

Although scholars have historically condemned the discipline of anthropology for being the handmaiden of colonialism, contemporary scholars need not continue to overly blame the discipline. While it is true that the discipline was used by colonists to further their ends, African scholars need to notice that the discipline is merely a tool and therefore it must not be blamed. What is bad is the way the disciplinary tool was used. The tool can very well be used in postcolonial Africa for beneficent ends to help Africa decolonise and develop. What is needed therefore is to adjust the discipline and turn it into a powerful apparatus for African liberation and scholarly growth.

In a context where transformation has become the battle cry, it is necessary to mobilise the discipline of anthropology in order to understand the ramifications for global transformation on Africans. Furthermore, in a world where there is not only resurgence of indigenous knowledges, but also where Euro-modernity is increasingly troubled, there is need to revive the discipline of anthropology that renders local 'alternatives'. Local 'alternatives' to western neoliberal economies need to be supported through anthropological researches; local anthropological jurisprudence need to be supported so that they provide 'alternatives' to western jurisprudence that is increasingly criticised for legal imperialism; local social security systems need to be supported through anthropological research since they provide 'alternatives' to faltering western social security systems. With increasing criticism being levelled on western NGOs/CSO that are deemed by many to be fronts for neo-imperialism, local 'alternatives' need to be supported through anthropological research. In short, the discipline of anthropology promises to endow the continent with richness that is crucial in a world where global capital is erasing 'alternatives' for humanities so that it continues to force them to dance to its planetary dictates.

The future of anthropology appears to be promising in the light of contemporary theoretical trajectories on decoloniality wherein Euro-modernist epistemologies and practices are challenged using local indigenous epistemologies and practices. In a world where theories on resilience and complexity are gaining traction particularly because they acknowledge the value of indigenous knowledges, practices and cultures, the future of anthropology is promising in Africa including in Zimbabwe. Important areas such as intellectual property Rights, emergent genetically modified food and organisms, global transformation, anthropology of science and technology studies, the value of herbs and organic foods and indigenous mining point to the value of anthropology in understanding and supporting African 'alternatives' to western imposed hegemonic systems.

Although some Africans fail to recognise the value of anthropological and indigenous knowledge and practices, institutions such as the World Health Organisation are recognising such indigenous knowledge and practices. The increasing contemporary popularity of circumcision, paradoxically after centuries of colonial condemnation, underscores that worldwide indigenous knowledge and practices are recognised. Thus while some Africans remain in the colonial mode of denial and demonization of indigenous knowledge, western institutions are benefiting from anthropological studies on circumcision and healing and medicine. The future of African and of the discipline of anthropology therefore lies in recognising the institutions, epistemologies and practices of Africans.

Thus, anthropological support of indigenous knowledge and practices promise the continent a future where humanity retains options in life. The discipline promises a future for Africans that is not threatened by what Chimamanda Adichie (2009) calls the "danger of a single story". This danger of a single story is traceable to the colonial single story of mission *civilisatrice* in which all that was African was demonised and deemed backward. Anthropology as a discipline promises to correct colonial misrepresentations of Africans, as desperately and hopelessly backward. In short, anthropology promises to enhance the relevance of academies for Africans with Africans.

An example of the promising future of anthropology is in the realm of development where for instance Africans scholars like Kwesi Prah (2011) and Mawere (2015) have argued that culture is the missing link in Africa's development. Whereas Euromodernist scholars have traditionally condemned African culture as unsuitable for development, the scholars argued to the contrary, that it is in fact the absence of culture that explains the failure of African development. Although African cultures including rituals, religions, family structures and so on continue to be vilified by some, such institutions are understood by others to be assets (Mararike 1999) for development. In fact Kwesi Prah argues that whereas in Africa

93

there is a gap between ordinary Africans and the bureaucrats in terms of the foreign languages used [by bureaucrats]; in the western countries the bureaucrats and the ordinary European people speak the same languages. These disjunctures can be followed up with further anthropological researches so that the development challenges of African can be effectively addressed.

The future of anthropology in Zimbabwe and the rest of Africa can be understood in terms of a number of developments. Firstly, if anthropology [in contrast to sociology] is defined as the study of non-industrialised societies, then anthropology promises to become more and more relevant to African societies that are deindustrialising since the inception of International Monetary Fund and the World Bank's neoliberal era. Africa since the neoliberal era has been losing industries, industries have been collapsing, industries have also been retrenching workers, the industries have become leaner and some have therefore become more mechanised than socialised. Some of the industries [in export processing zones] have in fact been deregulated and catapulted beyond the regulatory powers of African governments. With all these trends, African people have increasingly resorted to informal or non-formal sectors of the economy for survival, they have increasingly come to stay in squatter settlements that speak less to industrialisation than to deindustrialisation, Africans, particularly since the neoliberal era, have increasingly resorted to traditional medicines rather than to costly modern medicine. Thus, anthropology, being the study of non-industrialised societies, is becoming more relevant and conditions for its growth as a discipline are growing on the continent.

With rising levels of poverty and squalor in Africa, and with Africans increasingly living on the margins of industrialisations and on the basis of scavenging rubbish dumpsites, anthropology is best placed to study, understand and engage in the management of the necessary change. The discipline is best placed to resurface 'alternative' industrialisation; dwelling systems, food stuff, 'alternative' understandings of weather and climate; anthropology is best placed to study and understand 'alternative' mining and smelting systems. It is suited to resurface 'alternative' economies for which scholars at a global level are searching.

In Zimbabwe and the rest of African countries, there are currently manoeuvres for indigenisation of economies, knowledge systems and practices. Countries like South Africa, Namibia and Zimbabwe are indigenising their economies. In Zimbabwe indigenisation of industries, including mining and beneficiation, indigenisation of agriculture and education systems and medicinal systems have already started. Such indigenisation systems have implications for the future of anthropology. Anthropology as a discipline can resurface indigenous precolonial mining and smelting for purposes of enriching the debates and trajectories. Anthropology will resurface knowledge about precolonial industries and industrialisation for purposes of enriching the discourses and practices on indigenisation of industries in Africa. The current Black Economic Empowerment (BEE) policy in South Africa stands to be enriched by anthropological studies of Ubuntu for example and the ways in which it has played out with precolonial African industries. Similarly the indigenisation policy in Zimbabwe stands to benefit from anthropological studies on *chivanhu* and how it played out with and supported African precolonial industries.

In the light of the fallout between Africa and the International Criminal Court (ICC), anthropology provides a future for Africa given its relevance in studying and resurfacing 'alternative' African jurisprudence. Western jurisprudence still dominates in Africa decades after independence and so there are paradoxes in that while western backed NGOs and Civil Society Organisations claim to champion human rights and the rule of law, they are in fact championing age-old western domination on Africa. While legal systems in Africa claim to champion freedom and equality, they in fact champion western jurisprudential hegemony over Africa and the continent has increasingly become in Harry Englund's (2006) sense a "prisoner of western freedom". What this entails is the need to revive anthropological studies of African 'jurisprudence' so that colonial misrepresentations can be corrected and also 'alternative' jurisprudence can be resurfaced to help in the decolonisation and transformation of Africa.

If Africans are apprehensive of neo-colonialism and neo-imperialism in the constitution and practices of the International Criminal Court, there is similarly need to study from an anthropological point of view current developments in terms of what western scholars call 'earth jurisprudence' and their constitution of what they call an "Earth Court". The point is to study these developments in terms of and from the point of view of African anthropologies, to interrogate them using African anthropologies in order to assess whether they portray African lifeworlds or they are machinations of the new empire in Hardt and Negri's (2000) sense. So, anthropology promises, in the future, to be relevant not only in studying microscale, local societies but it is also relevant in studying the nexus between the local and the global; its future is in liberating

Africa by providing the grit for the intellectual crucible for liberation and decolonisation.

If global capital thrives on denying and closing off 'alternatives' for humanity, anthropology promises a future where 'alternatives' are (re)surfaced for humanity to choose from. From the mission of civilisation, colonialism preached that there was no 'alternative'; the mission of the International Monetary Fund and the World Bank preached that there was no 'alternative' to the neoliberal economies yet all these destroyed African systems and economies. The current trajectory by missionaries of the "New World Order" is that there is no 'alternative' but to establish a one world government dominated by western states, governments and capital, and in it Africans will have no governments and states of their own. Therefore the future of anthropology is in providing the 'alternatives' for humanity to choose from rather than to be captured in age old discourses on absence of 'alternatives'. Anthropology promises to generate interesting insights on the interfaces between local indigenous people and the emergent agenda of New World Order. Without anthropology the debates on these interfaces will be considerably impoverished. Anthropology will ruminate over questions such as how this emergent agenda of New World Order is affecting localities and indigenous people; what are the ramifications of the agenda on indigenous people; how can indigenous people react to this emergent agenda and so on.

In Africa, including Zimbabwe, western organisations have stressed individualism thereby breaking apart kinship systems and institutions that stressed collectivism. This destroyed' alternative' welfare systems based on kinship networks and this was designed to leave the NGOs and CSO as the only providers of welfare. African medical and health systems were destroyed leaving no 'alternatives' but colonial western systems; African industries were destroyed leaving no 'alternatives' but western industries; African religions were destroyed leaving no 'alternatives' but western ones; African education systems were destroyed leaving out western ones as providers; currently African food systems are being destroyed to leave no 'alternatives' but western corporations such as Monsanto. Western capitalism is busy destroying marriage systems and paradoxically creating humanoid sex robots, pornographic industries to trap and capture those that fallout of the marriage systems (Nhemachena 2016). Since anthropology offers possibilities to think outside the spaces of the capitalist western system, it provides a future full of 'alternatives' to western global capitalist apparatuses of capture.

The future of anthropology in Zimbabwe and Africa as a whole is not only in the realm of applied anthropology but also in theorising Africa. Anthropologists have largely continued since the early colonial era to use theories from the western academies often to misunderstand African lifeworlds (Jeater 2007; Amadiume 1987; Oyewumi 2013). In this respect, African scholars continue to rely on theories with concepts and categories that lack even indigenous equivalents. Although they claim such theories are African and useful in understanding Africa, it is necessary to question how African are theories that cannot even be translated into African vernacular or indigenous languages. Theories used in Africa need to have sound foundations in African indigenous languages such that even ordinary indigenous people would easily understand theories developed using their own concepts and categories. To impose theories and concepts is to visit violence on Africa yet this is what scholars so fond of uncritical borrowing of theories and concepts from western epistemologies have done for centuries.

Thus, to begin with, so far theories applied on Africa have presumed uncritically that Africa is poor when in fact it is rich in mineral resources, human resources, wildlife and in cultural endowments. Such theories are not the theories of the future in Africa because they do not begin theorising Africa from the historiography and position of Africa. Such theories continue to erroneously presuppose the need for civilisation and they ignore the history of industrialisation by precolonial Africans. Similarly, theories continue to be applied onto Africa, which erroneously presume that Africans have only been subsistence producers and never in their precolonial history engaged in commerce and trade. The future of anthropology in Africa has to correct such inimical and erroneous theorisations calculated to demean Africans and trap them in western (mis)constructions. Suffice it to say here that theoretical debates about constructivism or constructionism are equally misplaced in as far as Africa is concerned: westerners did not merely construct Africa but they misconstructed Africa and therefore it is germane to write in terms of misconstructivism or misconstructionism rather than engage in simplistic western founded debates on constructivism or social constructionism debates.

African anthropology needs to begin theorising from the position of Africa and not from the position and assumptions of the western academies. Theories that begin from western locus of enunciation hide more than they reveal; they hide the damage that the west visited on Africa for centuries; they portray as in constructionist debates and discourses the west as creators or constructors of African and in the process they hide the immense damage and destruction that the west caused and is causing on the continent. Although such theories on constructionism have reigned in the academies including African ones for decades now, it is imperative for critical and perceptive African scholars to notice that such theories are epistemic sleights of hand often designed to hide more than they reveal. In fact constructions are often made in order to destroy and therefore theories cannot be simplistically about constructionism without paying attention also to [neocolonial] destruction.

Future anthropology for Africa therefore need not be bogged down in western theoretical terrain such as about constructivism particularly when we are writing about a continent where the west has not necessarily constructed but destroyed institutions and lifeworlds of indigenous Africans. Anthropology need not be bogged down in terrain that presuppose that western epistemologies can and are representing the realities of Africans particularly on a continent that has since the colonial era been mistranslated, misrepresented and misconstrued. Discourses and theoretical trajectories by the west on constructivism hide the destruction of African families, cultures, identities, environments, religions and marriages since the colonial era.

Thus future anthropological studies of Africa need to go beyond western theories that focus on reality as socially constructed because in Africa colonial reality was not socially constructed but it was misconstructed and misrepresented as evidenced in scholarship on the crisis in representation that proliferated soon after independence in Africa. As far as the continent is concerned colonial social institutions did not necessarily construct social reality but it destroyed the social realities of Africans and such destruction continue in the postcolonial era. The challenge for anthropology of the future of the continent is to begin understanding African lifeworlds not from western theories but from African stories and experiences.

In a context marked by the ontological turn, future anthropology in Zimbabwe and Africa more generally has to ask deep ontological questions in addition to epistemological questions that have been asked anon. Scholars across the world have migrated to the ontological turn that is used to generate insights in science and technology studies; environmental studies, religious studies and so on. Thus in addition to asking questions about the nature of knowledge, there is also need to ask question about reality and how we come to know of it. In order to enter into dialogue with scholars from elsewhere who are debating ontologies and epistemologies, it is necessary that African anthropology in the future, researches on African ontological issues. If African anthropologists do not keep abreast with broader debates, they risk failing to engage in helpful debates about African ontologies and epistemologies. The risk is that ontological lessons from elsewhere will be imposed on Africa in much the same way colonial ontologies and epistemologies were foisted on the continent. Contemporary debates about personhood in relation to humanoid robots will potentially challenge African ontologies and epistemologies so African anthropologists need to enter into debates in order to correct ongoing (mis)representations about African ontologies.

Africa therefore needs an anthropology that will enable it to understand and resolve the problem that has resulted in Africans being displaced from Africa. The challenge that African institutions, cultures, identities, religions, economies, polities, resources have been displaced from Africa since the colonial era requires attention. The continent needs anthropology of the future that does not take epistemologies and ontologies for granted. It needs anthropology which privileges studying racism but also the self-hatred by Africans that has resulted for a long time in Africans becoming institutional refugees of others. In other words, the problem of the moment is not merely racism, it is self-hatred and self-pity induced partly by ossification of global racism that fortresses colonial *fait accompli* on the continent. What appears to be resolution of racial differences in the world is in fact an expression of self-pity and self-hatred particularly in a world where as Nyamnjoh (2016) notes Africans engage in whitening-up including using chemicals some of which ultimately damage their morphologies and skins. Future African anthropology needs to study such phenomenon of self-pity and self-hatred in addition to studying the hackneyed issues of racism.

Studies of displacement need not only focus on physical displacements of African bodies but also institutional, psychological and cultural displacements from the continent. In spite of numerous studies on displacements, some generously funded by western foundations, on displacements, there have not been any studies on the displacements of African institutions, psychologies, cultures and religions and resources yet these aspects and institutions should be at the core of anthropological inquiries. Anthropology in Africa need not privilege the [displaced] body only but also the institutions within which the bodies are located. Similarly, while studies of genocide have been done on the continent, there have not been studies on African cultural, epistemic, religious, family etc. genocides: pre-eminence has sadly been on genocides in relation to physical bodies.

What is needed in Africa is not merely critical anthropology or anthropology informed by critical theories but what is needed in an anthropology that reverses colonisation. In other words, what is needed are theories that reverse rather than ones that merely criticise and critique colonisation. To criticise is not enough because colonisation itself was not merely about criticising and critiquing African lifeworlds; rather colonisation was about reversing African lifeworlds and trajectories. The antidote to reversal cannot be mere critique; it has of necessity to be reversal. The point here is that while there has been in postcolonial Africa critical anthropology informed by critical theories, such critical anthropology is not *ipso facto* decolonial anthropology. Critical anthropology can only critique and engage in reformism of the (neo)colonial establishments; it does not reverse the establishments sufficiently for it to warrant the label 'decolonial' anthropology.

The future decolonial anthropology will be mindful that colonisation and coloniality is a mask dance in Achebe's (1986) sense. Much like in Achebe (1986: 46) where he argues: "The world is like a mask dancing. To see it well you do not stand in one place", African anthropologists need not stand in one place if they want to see the world mask dance well. Further much like in a mask dance, colonisers hide behind their victims, behind objects and events and this is what makes decoloniality tricky. It is tricky in the sense that much like in a mask dance and in beating a snake constantly moving its head and tail, one has to be pretty sure to hit the head because hitting the tail does not undo the global colonial mask dance. In fact this has been the problem with anthropologists that opposed colonialism: they opposed colonialism in the territories on the continent of Africa but they did not do much to end global colonialism or western indirect rule that has continues into what has come to be known as postcolonial Africa. This poses lessons for contemporary and future anthropologists on coloniality: coloniality cannot be meaningfully fought by chopping off the territorially-evident tentacles of global coloniality. Rather coloniality will be meaningfully fought by distinguishing the head and the tail, the head and the tentacles of global coloniality and then targeting accordingly. But of course like in a mask dance, coloniality would always want to shield [make invisible] its head and or ensure that those fighting it mistake its tail for the head so that it can easily [maintain its vitality or] revitalise. Thus African anthropology of the future has to be wary of fighting or hitting the tails of coloniality or its figments rather than the head [which may very likely be invisible and extraterritorial] of such coloniality (Nhemachena 2016d).

An anthropology that continues to teach Africans to be disproportionately critical of themselves, their institutions and nation states is not decolonial anthropology because in essence it continues to inculcate in Africans colonial senses of self-hatred. Similarly an anthropology that teaches Africans to neglect their history and situatedness in that history is not decolonial because it perpetuates colonial neglect of African history. What is needed for the future is an anthropology that cultivates awareness of history including colonial and enslavement of the continent; needed also is an anthropology that is attentive to the preponderating global machinations that continue to treat African institutions and leadership in the logics in which chiefs were treated [as inconsequential and nonentities] during the colonial. The anthropology of decolonisation must of necessity not begin theorising from the abstract western context or epistemologies but it must begin from African locales, practices, epistemologies and ontologies.

The challenge in rethinking Africa, using anthropology, is that much of the terms that are used in the academies and often uncritically applied are western and can therefore not easily render decolonisation unless critical analysis is employed. Terms and categories used emanate from a particular locus of enunciation and their meanings can therefore not be divorced from the context within which they originated. Ordinary Africans are seldom asked for their own terms and categories but they are required to define themselves using the borrowed terms and categories. The challenge is that uncritically foregrounding western terms and categories in trying to understand African anthropologies is like putting the intellectual cart before the horse. This, according to Jeater (2007) is why colonists mistranslated Africa, and one may add that this is how even uncritical Western trained Africans are still failing to understand Africa. The challenge as Nyamnjoh (2012) argues is that many scholars when they fail to understand Africa begin to excel in doing and writing irrelevance as they foreground terms and categories from other locus of enunciation.

To avoid the condemnation and bad reputation that it acquired as the handmaiden of colonialism, anthropologists in Africa have to avoid repeating colonial caricaturing of Africans as indistinct from animals, in terms of animism; they have to avoid colonial likening Africans to machines and technology. In other words, anthropologists of Africa's future need to avoid excelling at irrelevance and they need to seriously consider the Africans as humans.

The point here is that anthropology of the future in Africa has to excel not in irrelevance but in relevance on the continent. If colonial anthropology was relevant for the development of colonialism and patrimonialism, then anthropology in post-independence Africa has to be relevant first and foremost to the lifeworld of ordinary Africans that have sadly so far been promised vacuous freedom, emancipation and civilisation by both colonial and postcolonial governments and scholars. In future, anthropology on the continent need to be primarily focused on understanding Africans on their own terms rather than on modelling and engineering Africans towards the desiderata of funders and scholars of anthropological discipline.

The challenge for anthropology is well captured by Michael Crowder (1987: 110) cited in Ntarangwi *et al* (2006: 36) who noted thus: "…African lecturers 'are overburdened with teaching, do not have access to the latest books and journals, cannot obtain funds to travel to conferences outside their countries, and are unable to find funds even for local research".

Where African scholars rely on external funding, Ntarangwi *et al* (2006: 37) observe: "With almost all research being driven by local or international donors, anthropological work in Africa is unable to produce the contributions to ethnography, comparative theory and applied work necessary to sustain local scholarship and teaching-instead the main value of the work produced is to the specific funding agencies supporting it". So anthropologists like Ntarangwi *et al* (2006) argue that funding organisations such as the Ford Foundation, USAID, the Rockefeller Foundation, the Global Fund, the Norwegian Agency for Development Cooperation, Swedish International Development Agency, the World Bank and the International Monetary Fund exercise influence and condition the shape of anthropological writing, even within universities.

What this implies is the need to have autonomous well-funded African academies that can incubate the discipline of anthropology. In African where already the Bretton wood institutions like the International Monetary Fund and the World Bank have imposed deleterious neoliberal policies that wrecked the economies of African countries, government it will be unlikely that the governments will be able to fund anthropological research and even autonomous anthropological departments any time soon. The discipline will most likely remain captured by external funders who then call the tune for the pipers that have paid (Nyamnjoh 2004) and it will also remain captured in other departments that it will have to continue to subserve.

In the light of the recent FeesMustFall movement by students in South African and Namibian universities, income for public universities will further be eroded such that research and teaching disciplines such as anthropology will suffer further casualties. A number of universities in South Africa and Namibia have complained about dwindling sources of income and the possibilities that they, as universities, faced collapse. In this sense the future of disciplines such as anthropology remain grim unless African economies improve and governments are more willing to increase funding allocations for them. In fact increasingly academies and governments are preferring science, technology and mathematics in terms of funding and this threatens social sciences and humanities subjects including anthropology. This is of course unfortunate in that just as colonial administrations in Africa needed anthropology to support them, postcolonial African government need anthropology to decolonise and liberate Africa. Liberation cannot merely be technologically and scientifically driven just as colonisation was not simply technologically and scientifically driven. There is much more that is needed to decolonise, develop and liberate Africa in the twenty-first century, and that includes resurfacing African anthropology and putting it as much as possible to the service of Africans.

Chapter 7

Conclusion

This book, which reflects on the visibility, growth, vibrancy and future of the discipline of [social] anthropology in Zimbabwe, is timely and critical in a number of ways. It is a book penned at a time when the teaching of anthropology in Zimbabwe's academic corridors is waning yet most needed than any time before.

From the realisation that anthropology in Zimbabwe, as elsewhere in Africa, is dying a natural death, the book makes a notable observation that anthropology's growth as a discipline is both frustrating and disheartening. This sluggish growth is precipitated by the history of [social] anthropology which is mired with controversies of epic proportions, both as a brainchild and forerunner of colonialism. In fact, for many postcolonial governments of Africa, anthropology just like a friend of a thief who shares the latter's spoils, has been caught in between and betwixt colonialism and the genuine quest for understanding human societies and their cultures. As such, anthropology has become a prodigal son who needs to swiftly make up his mind and repent before it is too late to come back and re-join the family. Unfortunately, it has become difficult but never late for anthropology to dissociate and clear itself from the nefarious scheme of colonialism.

Yet, as has been clearly elaborated in this book, the unfortunate history of social anthropology should not be overemphasised to throw out the bath water together with the baby. There is need to salvage the sweet juice of anthropology as a complete science of men; a science of the whole. In fact, the indubitable role and continued relevance of anthropology in modern-day society should never be sacrificed. Neither should it be underestimated to make men surrender their destiny to the so-called natural sciences and the anthropocene; sciences which have always sought to exclusively monopolise the terrain of knowledge.

On this note, we have pushed the argument that the need to showcase the virtues and positive contributions of anthropology to the entire history, civilisation and knowledge of human society is more urgent now than ever. It is most critical at this moment when anthropology like a sacrificial lamb finds itself on the altar waiting for its final breath. It is on the same note that this book has considered as one of its objectives to reflect and understand the contextual history and trends existent in the [under-]development of Anthropology in Zimbabwe and beyond Africa's many nation-states. It has, for example, been demonstrated that the behaviour (as with culture in general) of a people is never haphazard but conforms to a pattern in the society as a whole. This knowledge, which no other discipline is privileged to access, can only be accessed through the lenses of anthropology, whose task is to understand in some profound details the societies of the world including their cultures and relationships therein. Likewise, while other disciplines such as philosophy and sociology study morals, it is only anthropology that managed to point out that the morals of other peoples are different, for a reason, from our own. It is anthropology that has and continues to save us from making false deductions from the popular theory of evolution which falsely captured that "the actions of the 'primitive' peoples represented a kind of natural behaviour" (Nida 1954: 48). As Nida have aptly showed us, such reasoning about relativity of behaviour is flawed as it has two basic errors:

i). It assumes that the 'primitive' man does behave naturally; and

ii). It assumes that one can transpose into one's own society all the factors in the factors in so-called primitive society which would in any measure justify such deeds

Departing from both the false deductions of the theory of evolution and Nida's acknowledgement of primitivism, we argue that as anthropological studies around the world have shown, all cultures are equal. There is neither superior nor inferior culture. It is total misunderstanding and [deliberate] misrepresentation of cultures and peoples of the world that Western scholars such as Aristotle, David Hume, Georg Hegel, Emmanuel Kant, John Stuart Mill, Levy-Bruhl and others, through their myth of superiority, have laboured to put the human race into categories of superiority and inferiority, civilised and primitive, logical and pre-logical, among other dialectics of the opposites on the assumption that the evolution of men encompasses cultural development which results in civilisation. Using the same argument we advance that *true* anthropology do not agree on the existence of "primitive men" for it is an enterprise that seeks to honestly and earnestly understand human societies without prejudicing any group of people. After all, isn't it that what one society considers as primitive is considered otherwise in another society? By whose measure then do those who labour to distinguish primitive societies from civilised society make their judgments? The relative relativism of culture is not only expressed by anthropology but unmistakenly enunciated even the Holy Scriptures. The Apostotle Paul, for example, attempted to be everything to all men that he might win some into the Kingdom of God. In 1 Corinthians 9:20-21, Paul thus says:

And unto the Jews I became as a Jew, that I might gain the Jews; to them that are under the law, as under the law, that I might gain the that are under the law; to them that are without law, as without law that I might gain them that are without law.

This means Paul's actions as with anthropology as a discipline is a recognition of cultural difference, which do not only influence standards and action, but should be respected. This is not to close room for growth, adaptation and freedom, for anthropology acknowledges that the relative relativism permits growth, adaptation and freedom under the law of society.

With the daunting of the force of anthropology both in the teaching and visibility of the discipline in the corridors of the academies of Zimbabwe and by extension Africa, the present text is critical to rekindle and rejuvenate the anthropological spirit of good faith. Like a searchlight which beams lushly, the book resuscitates the dying spirit of anthropologists and anthropology in the country and beyond.

References

AASA. (1987) Association for Anthropology in Southern Africa, *Ethical Guidelines*, Section 2 (i) & (ii).

Achebe, C. (1986) *Arrow of God*, Heinemann Educational Publishers: Oxford.

Amadiume, I. (1987) *Male Daughters, Female Husbands: Gender and Sex in African Society,* Palgrave Macmillan.

Amutabi, M. N. (2006) *The NGO Factor in Africa: The Case of Arrested Development in Kenya*, Routledge: New York.

Andrews, E. (2010) Christian missions and colonial empires reconsidered: A black evangelist in West Africa, 1766-1816, *Journal of Church and State,* Vol. 51, No. 4, 663-691.

Asad, T. *(Ed) (*1973) *Anthropology and the colonial encounter*, Ithaca: London.

Asante, M. K. (2000) T*he Egyptian Philosophers: Ancient voices from Inhatep to Akhenaten,* African American Images: Chicago.

Barrett, S. R. (1984) *The rebirth of Anthropological Theory*, University of Toronto: Toronto.

Baron, A. A. (2005) *Empire and Imperialism: A Critical Reading of Michael Hardt and Antonio Negri*, Zed Books: London.

Beach, D. N. (1994) *The Shona and Their Neighbours*, Blackwell Publishing: Oxford.

Bernard, P. (2007) Reuniting with the Kosmos, *Journal for the Study of Religion, Nature and Culture*, Vol. 1, No. 1, 109-129.

Bernard, P. S. (2003) Ecological Implications of Water Spirit Beliefs in Southern Africa: The Need to Protect Knowledge, Nature and Resource Rights, *USDA Forest Service Proceedings, RMRS-27:* 148-154.

Bhila, H. H. K. (1982) *Trade and Politics in a Shona Kingdom: The Manyika and Their Portuguese and African Neighbours 1572-1902*, Longman Group Ltd: Essex.

Bird-David, N. (1999) Animism Revisited: Personhood, Environment, and Relational Epistemology, *Current Anthropology* 40: S67-S91.

Blaser, M. (2009) Political Ontology. *Cultural Studies*, 23: 5, 873-896.

Bickerton, C. J. *et al.,* (2007) Introduction: The Unholy Alliance Against Sovereignty, in Bickerton, C. J. *et al,* (eds), *Politics without Sovereignty: A Contemporary International Relations*, Routledge: London and New York, p. 1-18.

Boas, F. (1928) *Anthropology and modern life,* Norton: New York.

Bourdillon, M. F. C. (1976) *The Shona People: An Ethnography of the Contemporary Shona with Special Reference to their Religion,* Mambo Press: Gweru.

Clifford, J. and Marcus, G. E. (1986) *Writing Culture: The Poetics and Politics of Ethnography*, University of California Press: Berkeley.

Clifford, J. (1988) *The Predicament of Culture: Twentieth Century Ethnography, Literature and Art*, Harvard University Press: Cambridge, Mass.

Boas, F. (1928) *Anthropology and modern life*, Norton: New York.

Bodley, J. H. (2001) *Anthropology and contemporary human problems*, Mayfield Publishing Company: California.

Fanon, F. (1963) *The Wretched of the Earth*. Grove Press: New York.

Latour, B. (2005) *Reassembling the Social: An Introduction to Actor-Network-Theory*. Oxford University Press: New York.

Nhemachena, A. *et al.,* (2016a) The Notion of the "Field" and the Practices of Researching and Writing Africa: Towards

Decolonial Praxis, in *Africology: The Journal of Pan African Studies* vol 9 (7)

Nhemachena, A. (2016b) '(Post-)Development and the Social Production of Ignorance: Farming Ignorance in 21st Century Africa,' In: Mawere, M. (ed), *Development Perspectives from the South: Troubling the Metrics of (Under-)development in Africa*. Langaa RPCIG: Bamenda.

Nhemachena, A. (2016c) Animism, Coloniality and Humanism: Reversing the Empire's Framing of Africa, In: Mawere, M. and Nhemachena, A. (eds), *Theory, Knowledge and Politics: What Role for the Academy in the Sustainability of Africa*. Langaa RPCIG: Bamenda.

Parekh, B. (1995) Liberalism and Colonialism: A Critique of Locke and Mill, in Pieterse J N and Parekh, B. (eds), *The Decolonisation of Imagination: Culture, Knowledge and Power*, Zed Books: London and New Jersey.

Bourdillon, M. F. C. (1991) *The Shona People*, Mambo Press: Gweru.

Bourdillon, M. F. C. (1999) 'The Cults of Dzivaguru and Karuva amongst the North Eastern Shona Peoples', In: Schoffeleers, J. (ed), *Guardians of the Land*, Mambo Press: Gweru.

Buchanan, R. and Pahuja, S. (2004) 'Legal Imperialism: Empire's Invisible Hand?', In: Passavant, P. A. and Dean, J. (eds), *Empire's New Clothes: Reading Hardt and Negri*, Routledge: London and New York, p. 72-92.

Bullock, C. (1927) *The Mashona (The Indigenous Natives of Southern Rhodesia)*, Juta and Co: Cape Town.

Bullock, C. (1950) *The Mashona and The Matabele*, Juta and Co Ltd: Cape Town

Burbridge, A. (1923) How to Become a Witchdoctor, *NADA: The Southern Rhodesian Native Affairs Department Annual* Vol 1: 94-100.

Burbridge, A. (1924) In Spirit Bound Rhodesia: *NADA* vol 1-6: 17-28.

Burbridge, A. (1925) The Witchdoctor's Power: A Study of its Source and Scope: *NADA*: 22-31.

Busia, K. A. (1962) *The challenge of Africa*, New York: Praeger.

Chavunduka, G. (1978) *Traditional Healers and the Shona Patient*, Mambo Press: Gweru.

Chavunduka, G. L. (1980) Witchcraft and the Law in Zimbabwe, *Zambezia*, Vol. VIII, No. ii, 129-148.

Chavunduka, G. L. (1994) *Traditional Medicine in Modern Zimbabwe,* UZ Publications: Harare.

Chavunduka, G. L. (2001) Dialogue among Civilisations: The African Religion in Zimbabwe To-Day, *occasional Paper No 1* Crossover Communication

Chirikure, S. (2010) *Indigenous Mining and Metallurgy in Africa,* Cambridge University Press: Cambridge.

Colson, E. (2006) *Tonga Religious Life in the Twentieth Century*, Bookworld Publisher: Lusaka.

Colson, E. (1971) *The Social Consequences of Resettlement: The Impact of the Kariba Resettlement upon the Gwembe Tonga,* Manchester University Press: Manchester.

Colson, E. (1962) *The Plateau Tonga of Northern Rhodesia: Social and Religious Studies,* Manchester University Press: Manchester.

Comaroff, J. and Comaroff, J. (2005) The Colonisation of Consciousness, in Lambek, M., ed, *A Reader in the Anthropology of Religion,* Blackwell Publishing: Oxford. 493-510.

Crossman, P. and Devisch, R. (1999) *Endogenisation and African Universities: Initiatives and Issues in the quest for plurality in human sciences*, Leuven: Katholieke Universiteit.

Crosson, J. B. (2013) Anthropology of Invisibilities: Translation, Spirits of the Dead and The Politics of Invisibility, *Cultural Fieldnotes*, http://prodn.culant.org/fieldsights/346-invisibilities-translation-spiritsof　　　-the-dead-and-the-politics-of-invisibility.

Daneel, M. (2007) *All Things Hold Together: Holistic Theologies at the African Grassroots,* University of South Africa.

Daneel, M. L. (1998) *African Earthkeepers,* Vol 1. Pretoria: University of South Africa.

Davies, C. A. (2009) *Reflexive Ethnography: A Guide to Researching Selves and Others,* Routledge: Abidon.

Dean, J. (2004) The Networked Empire: Communicative Capitalism and the Hope for Politics, in Passavant, P. A. and Dean, J. (eds), *Empire's New Clothes: Reading Hardt and Negri,* Routledge: London and New York p 265-286.

Diop, Cheikh Anta. (1974) *The African origin of civilization: myth or reality*, Mercer Cook (trans.) L. Hill: New York.

Ellert, H. (1984) *The Material Culture of Zimbabwe,* Longman Zimbabwe Ltd: Harare.

Ember, C. R. and Ember, M. (1990) (6th ed). *Anthropology*, Prentice Hall: New Jersey.

Englund, H. (2006) *Prisoners of Freedom: Human Rights and the African Poor*, University of California Press: Berkeley.

Escobar, A. (2002) Worlds and Knowledges Otherwise: The Latin American Modernity/Coloniality Research Programme, *Presented at the Tercer Congreso internacional de latino-americanistas en Europa*, Amsterdam.

Escobar, A. (1992) Imagining a Post development Era? Critical

Thought, Development and Social Movements, in Social Text No 31/32, *Third World and Postcolonial Issues:* 20-56.

Escobar, A. (1995) *Encountering Development: The Making and Unmaking of the Third World,* Princeton University Press: Princeton.

Escobar, A. (2002) "Worlds and Knowledges Otherwise" Latin American Modernity/Coloniality Research Programme, *Presented at the Tercer Congreso Internacional de Latin Americanistas en Europa,* Amsterdam, July 3-6, 2002.

Escobar, A. (2008) *Territories of Difference: Place, Movements, Life, Redes,* Duke University Press.

Falola, T. (2001) *Violence in Nigeria: The crisis of religious politics and secular ideologies,* University Rochester Press.

Farris, J. C. (1973) 'Pax Britannica and the Sudan: S. F. Nadel,' In: Asad, T. *ed, Anthropology and the colonial encounter,* Ithaca: London, p. 153-170.

Frazer, J. G. (1926) *The Worship of Nature,* MacMillan and Co Ltd: London.

Ganiage, J. (1968) *L'Éxpansion coloniale de la France sous la troisième République, 1871 1914,* Payot: Paris.

Gardner, K. and Lewis, D. (1996) *Anthropology, development and the post-modern challenge,* Pluto Press.

Gelfand, M. (1962) *Shona Religion with Special Reference to the Makorekore,* Juta and Co Ltd: Cape Town.

Gelfand, M. (1956) *Medicine and Magic of the Mashona,* Juta and Co Ltd: Cape Town.

Gelfand, M. (1959) *Shona Religion with Special Reference to the Makorekore,* Juta and Co Ltd: Cape Town.

Gelfand, M. (1959) *Shona Ritual with Special Reference to the Chaminuka Cult,* Juta and Co: Cape Town.

Gelfand, M. (1962) *Shona Religion with Special reference to the Makorekore*, Juta and Co Ltd: Cape Town.

Gelfand, M. (1964) *Witchdoctor: Traditional Medicine Man of Rhodesia*, Harvill Press: London.

Gelfand, M. (1966) *An African's Religion: The Spirit of Nyajena: Case History of a Karanga People*, Cape Town: Juta and Co Ltd.

Gelfand, M. (1967) *The African Witch: with Particular Reference to Witchcraft Belief and Practices Among the Shona of Rhodesia*, London and Edinburgh: E & S Livingstone Ltd.

Gelfand, M. (1970) Unhu-The personality of the Shona, *Studies in Comparative Religion,* Vol. 4, No. 1, www.studies in comparative religion.com.

Gelfand, M. (1981) *Ukama: Reflections on Shona and Western Cultures in Zimbabwe*, Gweru: Mambo Press.

Gelfand, M. (1985) *The Traditional Medical Practitioner in Zimbabwe*, Mambo Press: Gweru.

Gelfand, M. (1988) *Godly Medicine in Zimbabwe*, Mambo Press: Gweru.

Harrison, G. G. (1975) Primary adult lactase deficiency: A problem in anthropological genetics, *American Anthropologist*, Vol. 77 (1975): 812-35.

Hegel, G. (1956) *The philosophy of history (adopted from Hegel's Lectures* of 1830-1831*)*, Dover: New York. Available at: http://wssbd.com/wx/201503/a Does Africa really exist .html.

Herva, V. P. (2009) Living (with) Things: Relational Ontology and Material Culture in Early Modern Northern Finland, *Cambridge Archaeology Journal* Vol. 19, No. 3, 388-398. http://journals.Cambridge.org/CAJ.

Horton, R. (1967) African Traditional Religion and Western Science, *Africa,* Vol. 37, No. 1 & 2, 50-63.

Hountondji, P. (1983) *African Philosophy: Myth and Reality*, Henry Evans Trans. Bloomington: Indiana University Press.

Hymes, D. (1974) The use of Anthropology: Critical, political, personal, In: Hymes, D. *ed, Reinventing Anthropology*, New York: Vintage, p. 3-79.

Ingold, T. (2010) *Bringing Things to Life: Creative Entanglements in a World of Materials, ESRC National Centre for Research Methods:* Realities Working Paper # 15.

Ingold, T. (2008) Anthropology is not Ethnography, *Proceedings of the British Academy 154*, Oxford University Press: London, p. 69-92.

Jansen van Rensburg, N. S. (1994) Anthropology, social change and the reconstruction of South African society, *Koers* Vol. 59, No. 1, 3-18.

Jeater, D. (2007) *Law, Language and Science: The Invention of the "Native Mind" in Southern Rhodesia*, 1890-1930, Portsmouth: Heinemann.

Kenyatta, J. (1938) *Facing Mount Kenya; the tribal life of Gikuyu*, with an introduction by B. Malinowski, London: Secker and Warburg.

Kosek, J. (2010) Ecologies of empire: On the new uses of the honey bee, *Cultural Anthropology,* Vol. 25, No. 4, 650-678.

Kroeber, A. L. (1948) *Anthropology*, Harcourt, Brace and Company: New York.

Lan, D. (1986) *Guns and Rain: Guerrillas and Spirit Mediums in Zimbabwe*, Berkeley and Los Angeles: University of California Press.

Latour, B. (2004) Whose Cosmos? Which Cosmopolitics: Comments on the Peace Terms of Ulrich Beck, *Knowledge Commons,* Vol. 10, No 3, 450-462.

Latour, B. (1987) *Science in action: How to follow scientists and engineers through society*, Cambridge, MA: Harvard University

Press.

Latour, B. (2005) *Reassembling the social: An introduction to actor-network-theory,* New York, NY: Oxford University Press.

Latour, B. (1993) *We have never been modern,* Cambridge, MA: Harvard University Press.

Lentz, C. (1995) "Tribalism" and Ethnicity in Africa: A Review of four Decades of Anglophone Research, *Cali.Sci.hum,* Vol. 31, No. 2, 303-328.

Levi-Strauss, C. (1969) *The Elementary Structures of Kinship,* Boston, Eyre and Spottiswode (Publishers) Ltd.

Levi-Strauss, C. (1966) Anthropology: Its Achievements and Future, *Current*

Anthropology, 7.

Lewis, H. (2014) *Social and cultural anthropology and the study of Africa,* University Press:

Oxford, Available at: DOI: 10.1093/OBO/9780199846733-0141.

MacGonagle, E. (2007) *Crafting Identity in Zimbabwe and Mozambique,* Rochester:

University of Rochester Press.

Mafeje, A. & Wilson, M. (1963*) Langa: A Study of Social Groups in an African Township,* Cape Town, Oxford University Press.

Mafeje, A. (1963) *Leadership and Change in The Transkei (a Bantustan in the making),*

M.A. Thesis, Cape Town, University of Cape Town.

Mafeje, A. (1966) "The Role of the Bard in a Contemporary African Community", *Journal of Modern African Languages,* Vol. 6, Part II.

Mafeje, A. (1969) *Large-Scale Farming in Buganda. Society for Applied Anthropology,* University of California, Santa Cruz.

Mafeje, A. (1970) "The Ideology of Tribalism", *JMAS,* 9, 2.

Mafeje, A. (1971a) "The Fallacy of Dual Economies", *East African Journal,* 7, 9. Mafeje, A., 1971b. "What is Historical Explanation?"*African Religion Research*, University of California, Los Angeles.

Mafeje, A. (1976a) "The Land Question and Agrarian Revolution in Buganda", *in* W. Arens, Ed., *A Century of Change in Eastern Africa,* The Hague, Mouton.

Mafeje, A. (1977) "Neo-colonialism, State Capitalism, or Revolution" *in* P. Gutkind and P. Waterman. (eds), *African Social Studies*, London, Heinemann.

Mafeje, A. (1975) "Religion, Ideology, and Class in South Africa" *in* M. West and M. Whisson (Eds.), Jonathan Cape: Cape Town.

Mafeje, A. (1976b) "The Problem of Anthropology in Historical Perspective: An Inquiry into the Growth of Social Sciences", *Canadian Journal of African Studies*, X, 2.

Mafeje, A. (1978) *Science, Ideology, and Development,* Uppsala, Scandinavian Institute of African Studies.

Mafeje, A. (1998) Anthropology and Independent Africans: Suicide of End of an Era? *African Sociological Review* Vol. 2, No.1, 1-43.

Magubane, B. (1971) "A Critical Look at Indices Used in the Study of Social Change in Africa", *Current Anthropology*, 12.

Mamdani, M. (2011) The Importance of Research in a University, *Pambazuka*. http://pambazuka.org/en/category/features/72782.

Mawere, M. (2015) *Humans, other beings and the environment: Harurwa (edible stinkbugs) and environmental conservation in south-eastern Zimbabwe*, Cambridge Scholars Press: Cambridge.

Mawere, M. and Awua-Nyamekye, S. (Eds), (2015). *Harnessing Cultural Capital for Sustainability: A Pan Africanist Perspective*, Langaa RPCIG: Bamenda.

Mararike, C. G. (2011) *Survival Strategies in Rural Zimbabwe: The role of Assets, Indigenous Knowledge and Organisation*, Best Practices books: Harare.

Mudimbe, V. Y. (1988) *The invention of Africa: Gnosis, philosophy and the order of knowledge (African Systems of Thought)*, Bloomington: Indiana University Press.

Mudimbe, V. Y. (1994) *The idea of Africa*, Bloomington: Indiana University Press.

Muzvidziwa, V. N. (2006) The Teaching of Anthropology in Zimbabwe over the Past Forty Years: Continuities and Discontinuities, In: Ntarangwi, M. *et al.* eds, *African anthropologies: History, Critique and Practice.* Zed and CODESRIA: London, p. 99-113.

Nhemachena, A. (2013) Are Petitioners Makers of Rain? Rains, Worlds and Survival in Conflict Torn Buhera, Zimbabwe, Green, L. (ed), *Contested Ecologies: Dialogues in the South on Nature and Knowledge,* HSRC Press: Cape Town.

Nhemachena, A. (2016c) 'Social Support and the Violence of Individualistic Ontologies: Insights from Namibian Female and Male Youths' Experiences,' In: Mawere, M. *et al.,* (eds), *Myths of Peace and Democracy? Towards Building Pillars of hope, Unity and Transformation*, Bamenda: Langaa.

Nhemachena, A. (2016d) Double Trouble: Reflections on the Violence of Absence and the Culpability of the Present in Africa,' In: Mawere, M. *et al.,* (eds), *Violence, Politics and Conflict Management in Africa: Envisioning Transformation, Peace and Unity in the Twenty-First Century,* Langaa RPCIG: Bamenda.

Nhemachena, A. (2016b) 'Animism, Coloniality and Humanism: Reversing the Empire's Framing of Africa,' In: Mawere, M. and Nhemachena, A., (eds), *Theory, Knowledge, development and Politics: What Role for the Academy in the Sustainability of Africa?* Langaa RPCIG: Bamenda.

Nhemachena, A. *et al.,* (2016a) The Notion of the Field and the Practices of Researching and Writing Africa: Towards Decolonial Praxis, in Africology: *The Journal of Pan African Studies,* Vol. 9, No. 7, 15-36.

Nida, E. A. (1954) *Customs and cultures: Anthropology for Christian missions,* Harper & Brothers, New York.

Nkwi, P. N. (1976) *Traditional Government and Social Change,* Fribourg University of

Fribourg Press.

Nkwi, P. N. (1998a) "The Status of Anthropology in Post-independent Africa: Some Reflections on Archie Mafeje's Perceptions", *African Sociological Review, 2, 1.*

Nkwi, P. N. (1998b) *The Pan African Anthropological Association: Striving for Excellence,* Yaounde, Cameroon: ICASSRT.

Nkwi, P. N. (1989) *German Presence in the Western Grassfields.* The Netherlands: A.S.C. Leiden.

Nkwi, P. N. (2000) Anthropology at the University of Yaounde: A Historical Overview, 1962 –1999, in *The Anthropology of Africa; Challenges of the 21st Century,* Proceedings of the 9th Conference of the Pan African Anthropological Association, Yaounde: ICASSRT Publications (16-31).

Ntarangwi, M. *et al.,* (2006) 'Introduction: Histories of Training, Ethnographies of Practice,' In: Ntarangwi, M. *et al.,* (eds), *African Anthropologies: History, Critique and Practice,* Zed Books and CODESRIA: London and New York.

Ntholi, L. S. (2006) *Contesting Sacred Space: A Pilgrimage Study of the Mwali Cult of Southern Africa,* Eritrea: Africa World Press Inc.

Nyamnjoh, F. B. (2015) Beyond an Evangelising Public Anthropology: Science, Theory and Commitment, *Journal of Contemporary African Studies,* Vol. 33, No. 1, 48-63.

Nyamnjoh, F. B. (2004b) From Publish or perish to Publish and Perish: What Africa's 100 Best books tell us about Publishing in Africa, *Journal of Asian and African Studies,* Vol. 47, No. 2, 129-154.

Nyamnjoh, F. B. (2012c) Blinded by Sight: Divining the Future of Anthropology in Africa, *Africa Spectrum*, Vol. 47, No. 2-3, 63-92.

Nyamnjoh, F. B. (2012a) Potted Plants in Greenhouses: A Critical Reflection on the Resilience of Colonial Education in Africa, *Journal of Asian and African Studies*, Vol. 47, No. 2, 129-154.

Nyamnjoh, F. B. (2016) *#RhodesMustFall: Nibbling at Resilient Colonialism in South Africa,* Langaa RPCIG: Bamenda.

Nyamnjoh, F. B. (2004) A relevant education for African development: Some epistemological considerations, *Africa Development*, Vol. 29, No. 1, 161-184.

Nyamnjoh, F. B. (2006) Rethinking communication research and development in Africa, *CODESRIA Secretariat*, Dakar: Senegal.

Nyamnjoh, F. B. (2005) *Africa's media, democracy and the politics of belonging,* Zed Book, London.

Page, E. M. & Sonnenburg, M. P. (2003) *Colonialism: An international, social, cultural and political encyclopedia*, Vol 1. ABC-CLIO.

Posselt, F. W. T. (1935) *Fact and Fiction*, Salisbury: Government House.

Prah, K. K. (2011) 'Culture: The Missing Link in Development Planning in Africa,' In: Keita, L. ed, *Philosophy and African Development: Theory and Practice,* Dakar, CODESRIA.

Ranger, T. (1989) 'Missionaries, Migrants and the Manyika: The Invention of Ethnicity in Zimbabwe,' In: Vail, L. ed, *Creation of Tribalism*, Berkeley: University of California Press: 118-150.

Ranger, T. (1985) *The Invention of Tribalism in Zimbabwe*, Harare: Mambo Press.

Ranger, T. (2010) 'The Invention of Tradition in Colonial Africa,' In: Grinker, R. R. *et al.*, eds, *Perspectives on Africa: A Reader in Culture, History and Representation*, West Essex: Wiley-Blackwell.

SAHO, (2016) European missionaries in southern Africa, Available at: www.sahistory.org.za/article/europe/.

Said, E. (2006) *Orientalism: Western Concepts of the Orient*, Penguin Books: London.

Sawadogo, G. (1995) "L'avenir des universites africaines: mission, et role" paper presented at the Association of African Universities (AAU), Lesotho Conference.

Siamonga, E. (2016) Role of missionary churches in colonialism: Not all missionaries were that bad, *Patriot*, Harare.

Schmidt, E. (1992) *Peasants, Traders and Wives: Shona Women in the History of Zimbabwe, 1870-1939*, Heinemann: Harare.

Scholte, B. (1974) 'Toward a reflexive and critical Anthropology, In: Hymes, D., *ed, Reinventing Anthropology*, Vintage: New York, p. 430-457.

Scholte, B. (1981) Critical Anthropology since its reinvention, In: Kahn, J. S. and Llobera, J. R. *ed, The Anthropology of pre-capitalist Societies*, London: Macmillan, p. 148-184.

Turnbull, D. (2000) *Masons, Tricksters and Cartographers: Comparative Studies in the Sociology of Scientific and Indigenous Knowledge*, Amsterdam: Harwood Academic Publishers.

Verran, H. (2013) Engagements between Disparate Knowledge Traditions: Towards Doing Difference Generatively and in Good Faith, In: Green, L., ed. *Contested Ecologies: Dialogues in the South on Nature and Knowledge,* Cape Town, HSRC Press: 141-161.

Waite, G. (2000) Traditional Medicine and the Quest for National Identity in Zimbabwe, *Zambezia*, Vol. XXVII, No. ii, 1-33.

Werbner, R. (1989) Regional Cult of God Above: Achieving and Defending the Macrocosm, in Werbner, R. (ed), *Ritual Passage, Sacred Journey.* Washington: Smithsonian.

Werbner, R. (1991) *Tears of the Dead: The Social Biography of An African Family,* London: Edinburgh University Press.

Winch, P. (1964) 'Understanding a primitive society,' *American Philosophical Quarterly* 1: 307-324.

Wood, M. (2000) *Conquistadors*, BBC Publications.

Worsley, P. (1966) "The End of Anthropology?" *Sixth World Congress of Sociology*, May 1966.

Zeleza, P. T. (1997) *Manufacturing African Studies and Crises*, Dakar: CODESRIA.

Printed in the United States
By Bookmasters